# AMERICAN
# FASCISM

To Granddaughter
Lilley Pool

Granddad
Will Pool

# American Fascism

## A MEMOIR

WILL POOL

THE DEFEAT OF THE AXIS POWERS—Nazi Germany, Fascist Italy, and Tojo's Japan—during World War II did not destroy fascism as such. It merely took on a new dimension, more difficult to detect and combat effectively. This little paper is one old World War II vet's interpretation of the nature of the struggle against an internal enemy who controls, whether we realize it or not, every facet of our lives. I hope what I have presented proves provocative—a stimulus to action.

—*Will Pool, July 1, 2016*

# American Fascism

ONE OF MY FAVORITE WAYS TO GET PEOPLE'S ATTENTION, or to upset their equilibrium, is to state, "We lost World War II." Now everyone knows we were on the winning side of World War II, but what most have in mind is the military victory, not the attainment of the peacetime objectives for which we were fighting.

I usually continue the discussion of our country's loss of World War II by comparing the living conditions of present-day Germany with those of the United States. Suppose visitors from outer space landed on planet earth and were informed that two nations fought a vicious war against each other in which one emerged victorious as the strongest and most prosperous nation on the planet, while the other experienced disastrous defeat and massive destruction both human and material. Considering present-day appearance of our two nations, which nation would our visitors, assuming they were rational, judge to be the victor? The inevitable conclusion, of course, would be Germany.

Now I don't intend to make a detailed analysis of living conditions in the two countries, but I would like to make a few remarks. At the end of World War II, the United States emerged not only as the richest, most powerful state on the planet, but also as the most egalitarian of all the Western Nations and perhaps of those of the rest or the world as well. I recall hearing a remark recently, I think on NPR, that our egalitarian rank had slipped to somewhere between that of the Ivory Coast and Uganda. The only reason poor Americans live better than peoples of those countries is because of the huge wealth of our nation.

I have to deviate a bit from the United States–Germany victory question. A few more remarks are especially in order. Today, many young Americans choose to go to Germany to continue their higher education after completing secondary schools. In fact, Germany is the third most popular foreign country in which young Americans choose to study, outranked only by Canada and the U.K. Why Germany? Because, among other things, the tuition is free. (It might surprise you to know that tuition was also free in many of our public institutions of higher learning, before, and for a time after, World War II.) Also, Germany offers many amenities considered essential to present-day civilization. They have had national health insurance since the time of Chancellor Bismarck, in Kaiser Wilhelm's Germany of the 1880s. If one chooses to work in Germany, wages are considerably higher than those of the United States. Also, working conditions are better than those in the United States, due to the strength and rights of German workers to organize and bargain collectively without the hindrance of corporate management and a multitude of petty laws designed to undermine the strength of unions. Corporate books are pretty much open to German workers, and they gain quite a clear understanding as to what they may reasonably expect. I recall a German citizen also remarking, "No one works longer and harder than Americans." The working day and week, and time set aside for leisure, are much more clearly defined for Germans.

AT THIS POINT, THE QUESTION ARISES, "What were the peacetime objectives of the United States in World War II?" When the average American is asked that question today, what usually comes back is the vaguest answer, at best, or quite possibly no answer at all. Yet there really is no excuse for this reaction, since the peacetime objectives were real and clearly defined.

The clearest statement of what our peacetime objectives in World War II were was made by President Franklin Delano Roosevelt, in his State of the Union Address to the Nation on January 11, 1944. That statement contained what is often referred to as the "Second Bill of Rights." In brief, that Second Bill of Rights roughly contained eight basic points, including such concepts as: No more would one-third of the nation be ill housed, ill fed, and ill cared for, as had been the case when President Roosevelt took office in 1933. Instead, everyone was to be employed at a decent wage, under humane conditions, with adequate leisure. Care was to be provided for the sick and elderly, to ensure a sense of peace and security in the final years of their lives. Two of the most important items were provision for universal free access to health care, from "womb to tomb," and universal free access to education, from preschool through institutions of higher learning. Protection and promotion of the integrity of the family farmer along with small business was clearly implied. In essence, the Second Bill of Rights should be seen as an extension of gains made by ordinary people during the New Deal of the 1930s.

The Second Bill of Rights really was an extension of the "Four Freedoms" proclaimed by President Roosevelt in his State of the Union Address on January 6, 1941: Freedom of Speech, Freedom of Worship, Freedom from Want, and Freedom from Fear. The first two freedoms, of course, are contained in the United States Constitution, but the last two very much embody the spirit of the New Deal. The third freedom, "Freedom from Want," basically referred to economic opportunity, employment, social security, health, and education, which were to be given more detailed expression in the Second Bill of Rights. The fourth freedom, "Freedom from Fear," referred to some sort of international organization to ensure the peace and stability of the world for future generations.

The Four Freedoms played an important role in World War II as a means of focusing public attention on American values of freedom, economic opportunity, and human dignity and respect to which every individual was entitled, regardless of ethnicity, race, or gender. During the war, the famous painter Norman Rockwell gave a very inspiring visual representation of the Four Freedoms in paintings that were widely circulated in the *Saturday Evening Post* magazine. The Rockwell paintings are only one illustration of the impact the Four Freedoms had on focusing public attention and action behind the war effort. But the Four Freedoms were not a meaningless abstraction; along with the Second Bill or Rights, they represented objectives attainable within a generation. The Four Freedoms were also vigorously promoted by Eleanor Roosevelt and provided much of the inspiration for the U.N. Declaration of Human Rights in 1948.

AS MENTIONED PREVIOUSLY, the United States emerged at the end of World War II as the richest, most powerful nation on the planet, and certainly the most egalitarian of all the Western nations. One should add, we were probably the most literate as well. So what happened? How did we manage to slip in ranking? How did our one-time enemy, Germany, manage to outpace us in the basic elements of income distribution and livability?

The answer, I think, quite clearly lies in the failure to recognize the most difficult of all enemies—the internal one. Huey Long, the King Fish, the demagogic governor and senator from the State of Louisiana, author of the 1930s Share the Wealth Program, once said, "When fascism comes to America, it will come as pure, 100 percent Americanism." The greatest threat to American Freedom and Democracy was seen as some internal form of fascism.

How realistic was this assessment? For the answer to that question, I go to a statement made by Italy's former dictator, Benito Mussolini, an authentic author of "Fascism." When asked what fascism was, he simply answered, "It's when the corporations and government come together." Now, it's true that fascism contains much more than that. In Italy, as in Nazi Germany, Falangist Spain, Pinochet's Chile, and many other countries so afflicted, fascism has an elaborate superstructure. But its base is really that fundamental relationship of corporations to the government— a system devised to ensure economic, social, and political inequality for the benefit of a privileged few.

So what happened to that great egalitarian America that emerged from World War II? Why has it evolved into a state with rising inequality, homelessness, police brutality, mass incarceration, disintegrating infrastructure, a health system that doesn't begin to match the standards of other Western nations, and finally, a questionable educational system with student loans that condemn so many young people to a life of debt peonage? When considering indebtedness, what comes to mind is the old Scotch dictum passed from father to son: "Son, for every dollar you owe, you are that many times someone's slave." Debt peonage was one cause of the American Revolution. The revolutionaries of the time clearly recognized that indebtedness was clearly incompatible with freedom. They rebelled against the Bank of England and the British East India Company, and tried to bring money and interest under the control of the people, but were not very successful.

TO UNDERSTAND WHAT HAPPENED to the great egalitarian spirit and optimism that emerged out of the Great Depression and World War II, we have to look internally at the war effort itself. The war was to be "total war," meaning not just a military machine needed to do the fighting, but every facet of society—political, economic and social—and every individual was to be mobilized to support the war effort. This was to be a "People's War." Everyone was to sacrifice—not just the soldiers and sailors on the battle fronts.

Shortages of civilian goods and services were created as the means of production and distribution were drafted into the war effort, and so we had rationing. We made victory gardens to supplement the food supply. Old clothes were patched for continuous use. New ones were not readily available or easy to find. We had scrap-metal drives. Several of us boys bought an old 1920s sedan for $10 and donated it to the scrap metal drive. It still ran and so we drove it to the junkyard. We did our patriotic duty.

We were experiencing inflation, so taxes went up. For the first time, most Americans paid income taxes. A system of automatic payroll deductions was instituted to collect the taxes. Tax rates at the top were pegged at about 95 percent. War profiteering supposedly was out. We were urged to buy war bonds, and did. It was our patriotic duty. One didn't see many flags—people were too busy; just a gold star now and then, where somebody had lost a loved one in the fighting.

But was the sacrifice equal? Were war profits eliminated or at least severely curtailed? Everyone suffered from inflation. Workers' wages failed to keep up with the cost of living. There were strikes. The regular media—newspapers, magazines, movies and radio—condemned the strikers as unpatriotic. Government action was taken against them. The strikes were short and often legally banned. Workers were given some concessions to alleviate the financial problems and to smooth over some of the more severe working conditions caused by long hours and the speed-up involved in the effort to meet production goals. There was a labor shortage, and after the Great Depression most people were glad to have the work, even with the long hours. Vast new housing projects were built to meet the demographic changes caused by the war effort. Some of those projects still exist today, although they were only meant to last 10, or at most, 20 years.

With everyone working, what happened to business—to the great corporations that dominated our economy? They became greater. Their marriage with the government and the demands of the war effort made them very profitable. There was an excess profits tax, but business and industry were guaranteed profits from the war effort. The right to profit was a demand of business and industry if they were to cooperate in the war effort, and that right was built into the war planning structure. I don't know for certain what the rate of profit was, but the figure I heard most often was cost plus 10 percent. Now, that's interesting, because the higher the cost, the greater the profit. I can't help but reflect on the huge waste around the shipyards of Seattle and Tacoma, Washington. All of us were well aware of the use and abuse that went with war contracting.

People did not like what they saw, and the message soon got to Congress. The result was the creation of a senate investigating committee to look into the charges of abuse in war contracting. Harry Truman, junior senator from Missouri, was put in charge of that committee, and it soon operated under the name, "Truman Investigating Committee." Harry Truman was very energetic, and traveled thousands of miles to investigate contracting abuse charges at various factories, plants, and military facilities. Truman became very famous nationally and even appeared on the cover of *Time* magazine.

PROFITEERING HAS ALWAYS BEEN A PART of every war effort. As one former head of the United States Marine Corps, Smedley Butler, put it, "War is a racket." World War II was no exception, especially with cost-plus written into contracting. World War II is often referred to as "The Good War," because of the vicious nature of fascism, and in particular because of the genocidal proclivities of Nazi Germany and the absolute necessity of destroying it, if democracy was to survive in any form.

The rise of Nazi Germany was not some kind of historical accident. In the 1920s, Hitler once said, "If we are to succeed, we must adopt the techniques of American advertisers"—and so they did, and very successfully. Hitler had a very good understanding of corporate culture. The Nazis did not come to power in Germany through a coup, but through the electoral process and normal parliamentary means. They were part of a right-wing coalition that had the backing of Germany's most powerful businessmen and corporations; corporations like Krupp, Thyssen, and IG Farben. They had the financial wizardry of Hjalmar Schacht, who ended Germany's inflation of the 1920s and was set to play a crucial role in the economic recovery of the 1930s under Nazi leadership.

Nazi Germany provoked much admiration abroad, particularly among businessmen and the corporate elite. The first thing the Nazis did was to break up trade unions and destroy all possible forms of opposition on the left. This pleased American corporations and businessmen immensely. The opportunities for investments and profits in Germany were great. American corporations and business people became the largest foreign investors in Nazi Germany. Names like Ford, General Motors, and Du-Pont became part of the scene.

Now this should not surprise anyone who knows the answers to questions such as, "What is a corporation? How is it organized? What is its purpose?" A corporation as we think of it is primarily an economic institution, but it also has social and political aspects as we know only too well. It is a totalitarian institution with a top-down system of organization and management that continues on down until it reaches workers at the lowest level. The purpose of the corporation is to make money—to profit as much as possible. To profit, it needs a stable environment for investors. Authentically democratic countries with a strong populist element do not provide that atmosphere. In fact, they tend to be somewhat chaotic. And so they must be avoided or reformed in a more authoritarian direction if the corporation is to function and profit.

THINKING BACK TO MY BOYHOOD IN THE 1930S, there were a lot of fascist or ultra-rightist organizations in our country operating very much in the open. Among the organizations were the Ku Klux Klan, Silver Shirts, and the German American Bund. The Bund was even strong enough to completely fill Madison Square Garden—the nation's largest arena—with demonstrators dressed like people in similar events in Nazi Germany and waving flags emblazoned with the Nazi emblem—the Swastika.

I remember Mrs. Ehrlich, a neatly groomed and dressed lady of 50 or so, who was a secretary in a real estate office, once said to me, "Wilbert, if you have an ounce of German blood in your veins, it is your duty to support the Reich." The sympathizers with Nazi Germany were not scrubby skinheads or tattooed motorcycle riders, but for the most part conservative, middle-class people. Even Charles Lindberg, after being entertained by Herman Goering, Head of the Luftwaffe, came back with glowing reports of the country.

World War II, then, seemingly marked the victory of the freedom-loving democratic forces of the United States and its allies over the evil axis of Nazi Germany, Fascist Italy, and Emperor Hirohito's Japan, along with their puppets and sympathizers. The extent of the Allied Forces' commitment to freedom and democracy was somewhat questionable, however, as some minor fascist states, like Francisco Franco's Spain and Antonio Salazar's Portugal, were allowed to exist.

I WAS HOME ON LEAVE, AUGUST 6, 1945, when the atomic bomb was dropped on Hiroshima, Japan. Like everyone else, I realized the war was over, and I joined in the frenetic celebrations in downtown Seattle. The experience was unlike any I have had, before or since. It seemed most everyone—even the most austere—lost their inhibitions with all the hugging and kissing, shouts of joy, bottles of beverages, and food (lots of popcorn) being passed around for everyone's enjoyment. I remember catching a brief glimpse of my father in an opening, but then he quickly disappeared into the crowd. I also bumped into my eldest sister, who had been widowed twice during the war, but then she also disappeared. Or perhaps it was I who was lost! Everything was such a mass of confusion.

It's fun to reflect back on that time of such great excitement and hope, though over the years I came to feel the deepest regret imaginable for the destruction of Hiroshima and Nagasaki. And we knew little at that moment how the Yalta and Potsdam agreements would set the tone for years to come. In actual fact, the bombing of Hiroshima on August 6, 1945 was the opening shot of the "Cold War." It was unnecessary. The Japanese fleet and air force had been destroyed. Japan's major cities and transport centers were in ruins. It is arguable that the fire-bombing of Tokyo caused more damage, death, and injury than Hiroshima. In addition, Russia's entry into the war would take care of what was left of the Japanese army in Manchuria and Northeast China. One needs to note that there was much shock and disagreement over the use of the atomic bomb, not only among elements of the scientific community, but also among some of the top military commanders—most notably Air Force Commander Henry A. Arnold and Fleet Admiral Halsey. The latter was furious about the use of the bomb.

Someone once asked me if Roosevelt, had he lived, would have authorized the use of the bomb. I don't think so, at least not on a human target. He might possibly have authorized a demonstration elsewhere of the bomb's power, but not on humans. He was far too compassionate. This vast difference between Roosevelt and Truman has been made clear over and over again in innumerable circumstances.

The question arises then, if it was unnecessary, why was the bomb used? The answer comes out of the Potsdam and Yalta agreements. At Yalta, Russia agreed to come into the Far Eastern War three months to the day after the war in Europe ended. The war in Europe ended on May 8, 1945, which meant Russia was to enter the war against Japan on August 8, 1945.

The explosion of the atomic bomb at the Trinity Site in New Mexico on July 16, 1945, changed everything. The Potsdam Conference, which was to further define the nature of the peace, opened on July 17, 1945. The initial opening of the conference was quite cordial between the three top leaders, President Harry Truman, Prime Minister Winston Churchill, and Marshall Joseph Stalin. All that changed on July 19, 1945, when President Truman and the American delegation got word of the successful explosion of the atomic bomb in New Mexico. President's Truman's attitude toward the Russians became quite arrogant and dictatorial. Rather quickly, President Truman came to the decision to use the atomic bomb on the Japanese as a means to hasten the end of the war before the August 8 deadline at which the Russians were to enter the war in Asia. In this manner, the United States would not have to share the occupation of Japan with the Russians, as had occurred with Germany.

The development of the atomic bomb and the destruction of Hiroshima and Nagasaki in August 1945 completed the emergence of the United States as the dominant power on the planet, with overwhelming military, industrial, economic, social, and political strength.

THE SOVIET UNION—Soviet power—was certainly depicted as a major threat to America—to our democracy and our way of life—by our political leaders and mainstream media of the time. Was it really a serious challenge? The answer is, Soviet Russia was not.

Most Americans have no knowledge, no real understanding of the terrible destruction the Russians experienced during World War II. The Russians bore 80 percent of the cost of the European phase of World War II. Two thirds of the European part of Russia experienced massive devastation. In fact, it was turned into a virtual desert. Central Russia was a free-fire zone. It's impossible to conceptualize the death and destruction experienced by the people of this region. In the end, the Russians lost 27 million people and experienced unimaginable suffering during that war.

Now there is a curious thing about how we opened the Western Front in Normandy, France in June 1944. Initially, we had indicated we would try to open a Western front in 1942, but that was unrealistic. A promise was then made to open a front in 1943, but that experienced a series of delays. Some reports lay the blame for the delay on Britain, primarily on Winston Churchill.

But there is an additional explanation, and that has to do with the deep suspicion and hostility, in this country and in Britain, held by powerful economic, social, cultural, and political groups toward Soviet Russia's experiment in socialism. The basic philosophy of these people was, let them bleed. And so the Russians bled.

The June 1944 invasion of Normandy became an absolute necessity for the Western Allies. The decisive event of the European phase of World War II was the Battle of Stalingrad, 1942–1943, which turned the tide of war in favor of the Russians. But the opening of the Western Front in June 1944 was absolutely necessary to the Western Allies, if they were to prevent the occupation of much of Europe by the Russians. The Russian recovery from defeat and their march toward victory had astonished most intelligence experts in the West.

THE TRANSFORMATION THAT TOOK PLACE in the United States as a result of World War II bears a very sharp contrast to that which the Russians experienced. Officially, we lost 404,000 in the fighting, plus six civilians on the Oregon coast. The U.S. economic engine expanded exponentially, with large corporations like General Motors, General Electric, Ford and DuPont devouring smaller entities into their network. Along with this development came the explosive growth of the aircraft industry, including corporations like Boeing and Martin-Marietta (Rockwell-Martin), which were pretty much in their infancy in the 1930s. In 1938, I joined Boy Scout Troop 140 in Seattle's University District. Besides usual troop meetings and hiking, skiing and camping, we also visited some local businesses and industries. One of the latter was Boeing Aircraft Corporation. It was located in a barn in south Seattle. The entire tour of the plant didn't take more than an hour or two.

The one really big outcome of World War II was the emergence of the military-industrial complex in the United States. There was never any plan on the part of key people in government, in the corporate structure, or in the military, to disarm after World War II. On the contrary, the desire was not just to maintain the armed might, but to improve and expand it. The military-industrial complex was to provide the shield behind which U.S. business and industry could function and expand. By its very nature, the military-industrial complex was to exert some influence on every aspect of American life, and upon the lives of millions of people far beyond the boundaries of the United States.

World War II put an end to the New Deal and, along with it, its expansion through the Second Bill of Rights. Basic measures such as social security, the right of workers to bargain collectively with management, the eight-hour day, and support by the federal government for the development and improvement of infrastructure projects such as roads, waterways, and schools were retained and improved upon, but the social and aesthetic characteristics of the New Deal evaporated. There were no more writers' and artists' projects, and none of the craftsmanship that marked projects like our Timberline Lodge on Mt. Hood.

Conservative elements, of course, hated the New Deal. They feared the populist spirit would overturn the established structure of American society, and along with it, the power and privileges of the elitist upper strata. But they were not alone in their hatred of the New Deal and New Dealers. Key elements of the Democratic Party also thoroughly disliked the New Deal and its activist promoters. The New Deal functioned in a manner that threatened the bureaucratic power and privileges that came to them as party officials and office holders.

President Roosevelt's popularity allowed him to go outside the party apparatus and search for and find people of talent and ability, whoever they might be, to bring into the New Deal government and its many projects. And so a good lone Republican of populist views like Henry Wallace was brought in as Secretary of Agriculture in an effort to keep the family farm afloat. Francis Perkins, a woman of socialist tendencies, was brought in as Secretary of Labor. She was the first woman to hold a top secretarial post in the U.S. government. Mariner Eccles, a conservative Mormon banker from the State of Utah, was appointed Chairman of the Federal Reserve Bank. Eccles felt strongly that the Great Depression was caused by an unequal distribution of wealth and income. And so the New Deal progressed.

NOW ALL THIS BRINGS US TO THE NATIONAL CONVENTION of the Democratic Party in 1944, which has been termed by some as the most Byzantine event in American political history. What the Democratic Party insiders knew, that outsiders and the rest of the American people didn't know, was that President Roosevelt wasn't just sick; he was a dying man. Whoever was selected as his vice-presidential running mate would be the next president of the United States. The insiders fervently wanted someone they could control.

At this point we need to take a look at which candidates were the most popular among the rank-and-file supporters of the Democratic Party. According to a Gallup poll, by far the most popular person was Henry Wallace, with about 65 percent support. Senator Alben Barcley followed, with 17 percent, then House Speaker Sam Rayburn with 5 percent, and way down towards the end, Senator Harry S. Truman, with 2 percent.

Now most anyone would have thought Vice President Wallace would have been a shoo-in for a second term with this support. President Roosevelt had personally elevated Wallace from Secretary of Agriculture to the vice presidential spot in 1940 because of Wallace's effectiveness in dealing with the very concrete problems facing the nation's farmers during the Great Depression. Wallace may have been popular with the people, but he certainly was not popular with the insiders in the Democratic Party. He was not controllable. They hated him.

Among the insiders was the president's personal secretary—the man who controlled access to the president. His function was to keep people like Wallace as far from the president as possible, and grant ready access to people of whom the insiders approved. People like Harry Truman were frequently mentioned or even presented to the president with their merits and abilities magnified. President Roosevelt was far too busy with the war and the nation's troubles to devote much if any attention to the forthcoming election of 1944. Those with ready access to him kept mentioning the name—Harry S. Truman—and how he would be more effective than Wallace as a running mate, since Wallace nationally was a more controversial figure. President Roosevelt at first endorsed Wallace, and probably more or less assumed he would be his running mate, but finally he gave in to the entreaties of the insiders and, in passing, endorsed Truman. And so the fate of the nation—and, one might add, the world—was decided.

THIS BRINGS UP THE QUESTION, who was Harry S. Truman? Basically, Truman began as a poor Missouri farmer. In many respects, Truman was a typical Missourian. Missouri had been a border state during the Civil War. Slavery was legal there, but Missouri did not cede from the Union. On Truman's father's side, the people had been free soil farmers. They owned no slaves. On Truman's mother's side, the family had a much more southern orientation. They had owned slaves. Somehow, when I think of Harry S. Truman, I think of events that took place in Ferguson, Missouri, this past year. Truman had the habits, attitudes, and prejudices typical of rural and small-town Missourians.

Truman was a small man with very poor eyesight. As a child, he had to wear heavy, thick glasses to compensate for his eyesight deficiencies. This, along with his small size, kept him out of the rough-and-tumble sports common to Missouri boys. He was afraid of being called a sissy. To some extent, he compensated for his physical shortcomings by becoming heavily addicted to reading. Of special interest to him were works on history, especially stories of great men like Alexander the Great, Napoleon, George Washington, Andrew Jackson and, of course, Ulysses S. Grant and Robert E. Lee.

Truman had an excellent memory—some even say a photographic memory. Truman managed, despite his physical deficiencies, to make a place for himself among his peers. He managed to gain their respect through his histrionic abilities, and by telling them stories of the great men whose lives he knew well and perhaps whom he really wanted to emulate.

World War I gave Truman the break he needed to depart from Missouri farm life. It gave him a chance to develop and use his oratorical and social abilities. He was an ardent supporter of the war and joined the Missouri National Guard. His fellow guardsmen elected him first lieutenant—a position of some significance, given that, in those days, in some states, including Missouri, guardsmen elected their own officers. Truman's election to the rank of first lieutenant was indicative of his ability to gain the confidence of his peers and, later, the public at large

Truman's service in World War I was to determine the future course of his life and make him the man he later became—a fact he readily admitted. That experience separated him once and for all time from the life of the Missouri farmer. While serving in the army in World War I, he became acquainted with a relative of Boss Pendergast, head of the Kansas City Missouri Democratic Party political machine. It was through Pendergast that Truman was formally introduced to the organization and operation of the Democratic Party in the government and politics of Missouri.

It wasn't long before Truman left the arena of local politics and made a run for the United States Senate. Initially, there wasn't much to distinguish Truman from other Democrats in the senate. By and large, he supported New Deal measures, and was one of the very dependable party faithful. Once again, war opened up a number of great opportunities for Harry S. Truman. As mentioned previously, it was his role as the head of a committee investigating corruption in war contracting that thrust him into the national limelight. That, along with his party faithfulness, made him the darling for the vice-presidential spot at the National Convention of the Democratic Party in 1944.

The Democratic Party of 1944 was no longer the vibrant populist party of the New Deal Era. It was an apparatus, more conservative, thoroughly under the control of party regulars whose primary objective, as always, was to maintain its position and power. It was at this time that Secretary of the Interior Harold Ickes complained to Vice President Wallace that it seemed they were the only two liberals left in the government.

I WILL NEVER FORGET APRIL 12, 1945, the day President Roosevelt died of a massive cerebral hemorrhage. I was walking along the seaplane ramp at the Corpus Christi Texas Naval Airbase when someone stopped me and excitedly exclaimed, "Have you heard the news? President Roosevelt is dead." My first reaction was one of disbelief—"What do you mean, dead?" President Roosevelt was the only president I had ever known. In my own mind, he couldn't die. At first, I discounted the news as just another nasty Republican rumor. But it was true—he was dead. Like many Americans, I was stunned.

It's hard to think of any two men much more different than Franklin Delano Roosevelt and Harry S. Truman. President Roosevelt had that semi-aristocratic Northeastern accent and the cultural bearing of his upper-class origins. He had that certain finesse and dignity that automatically attracted one's attention. Truman, on the other hand, had the down-to-earth speech and manner that made him so much a part of the Middle West. In many respects, he was the common man, and in that characteristic lay his great strength. He had the capacity to take complex issues and put them in a language understood by most everyone.

Unfortunately, there was little communication between President Roosevelt and Vice President Truman before President Roosevelt passed away. An ailing President Roosevelt was completely tied down by the burdens of his office, in particular the war effort, as he was heavily involved in both planning and execution. Obviously, he didn't have a great deal of confidence in Truman, failed to keep him informed, and in particular, Truman was given no information on the atomic bomb, its development and possible use.

Thus it was that Harry Truman entered the office of the presidency woefully ignorant of the procedures of governance. The blame certainly cannot be placed entirely on President Roosevelt. Truman made very little effort to inform himself, despite the deep-seated uneasiness he felt about his position, and in some sense about President Roosevelt's frail condition. Like most Americans, he felt great respect for the President and had difficulty imagining himself in the office held by that Great Man. The notification of President Roosevelt's death came as an indescribable shock to Truman.

SO HOW WAS TRUMAN TO RECOVER from this awesome event and assume the enormous burdens of the most powerful position in the world, in the midst of the greatest war that had ever been fought? Truman certainly was not lacking in ability and self-confidence. He stated bluntly that he was going to be the "president of all the people." In regard to his responsibilities, he made the statement, "I am here to make decisions, and whether they prove right or wrong, I am going to make them." Subsequently, Truman made decisions that to a large extent determined the nature of the world in which we live today.

He did not hesitate in assuming the business of government and the responsibilities for conducting the war. So far as the conduct of the war was concerned, he saw no need to make any serious changes. Truman was an ardent patriot and champion of the war effort. After all, it was war—World War I, more than anything else—that made him the man he was, something he readily admitted, as previously indicated.

Dealing with the ordinary, mundane business of government was a different matter. While a supporter of the New Deal, he was first and foremost a party loyalist. Obviously, many of the persons filling high office positions did not fit with his style of thinking and working. In one way or another, persons who had held key positions in he Roosevelt Administration were forced out of government. Six months after Truman took office, Secretary of the Interior Harold Ickes was leaving. Upon departing, he said to his long-time friend and current Secretary of Commerce, Henry A. Wallace, "Henry, you are the last of the old guard. You won't last six months." Ickes was wrong. Wallace lasted just six months before departing. The cleansing of the last of the Great New Dealers was complete and the country was to head down a different road. The changes were not the product of some conscious plan, but the outcome of the habits, attitudes, and mentality of Harry S. Truman and those around him, coupled with the momentous times through which we were all living.

There have been times when I have been tempted to label the advent of "Trumanism" as a coup d'état, but that would imply something of a sudden and violent overthrow. Instead, Trumanism represented a decline of the New Deal spirit and the slow erosion, under right-wing pressure, of the gains made during that period. Truman acknowledged the importance of the leadership of "that Great Man," as he referred to President Roosevelt, but lacked the vision or incentive to aggressively fight the Right—in Rooseveltian terms, the ability to say, "Let them hate me! I want their hatred."

Businesses prospered and profited as never before during World War II. Personal income taxes were high, but corporate taxes were not. Corporations were allowed to retain a goodly supply of their profits in their treasuries, and at the end of the war, in 1946, emerged on the political scene with buckets of money to influence the elections. The result was, the Democrats lost control of Congress, and further advances along New Deal lines were not possible.

With people like young Richard Nixon and the infamous Senator Joseph McCarthy in Congress, virtually anyone with liberal or progressive views—in particular-New Dealers—were objects of hysterical right-wing assault. Truman displayed occasional militancy in efforts to counter these attacks, but gave into the pressure and required government employees to take loyalty oaths, which the more scrupulous and honorable employees refused to do. Usually, such employees were promptly fired and often blacklisted, an action that impaired their future careers. The result was that most of President Roosevelt's Second Bill of Rights was never realized—things like universal health care, free education from preschool through college, extension of social security, public housing and aid to small farmers.

Worst of all was the assault on organized labor. Postwar inflation had resulted in a series of strikes, which rather seriously disrupted everyday life and produced some shortages of goods. Congress reacted by passing the Taft Hartley Act of 1947, which severely restricted the activities of organized labor. The result was the erosion of labor's power, and the gradual growth of inequality among the American people. As wealth became more concentrated at the top of the social pyramid, grassroots democracy was more and more undermined.

Nevertheless, the 25 years or so after World War II is often referred to as "The Golden Age of Capitalism." During the war, Americans were urged to save, and to buy war bonds as a means of keeping the rate of inflation under control. So now they had money to purchase the new goods and services coming into existence with the war's end. Most importantly, with much of Europe and Japan in ruins, there were no competitors for American goods. Postwar reconstruction and relaxation of trade restrictions created a huge demand for American goods, and created a tremendous opportunity for American investors. Fear of another depression was largely dispelled.

The post-war changes brought about under the leadership of Harry Truman did not come about smoothly or without serious challenges. Of particular concern was the breakdown of relations with our former great ally, the Soviet Union. Leadership in the State Department and the War Department (Defense Department) lacked the smoothness of Cordell Hull and Henry Simpson of the Roosevelt years. A clear sign that the old system of negotiation, cooperation, and compromise was gone was the statement made by Winston Churchill in his famous "Cold War speech," given in Fulton, Missouri, on March 5, 1946. In effect, Churchill accused Russia of throwing down an "Iron Curtain" across Eastern Europe and being set on a course to gain preeminence in the post-war world. Churchill gave no real recognition to the fact the Russians, having been invaded three times in 35 years from the West, had legitimate security concerns of their own.

President Truman rather passively sat and listened to the speech, applauded at the end, and did not bother to make much of a comment on it. Evidently, for the most part, he was in agreement with it. Thus the post-war Anglo-American alliance and system of cooperation, which would continue to the present, was formed. It should be borne in mind that Churchill's overriding objective was always to maintain the British Empire, and if that was not feasible, to maintain as much of its power and influence as possible, even if it meant subordination to the United States.

IN MAY 1948, 22 OF US STUDENTS AT Central Washington State College (now Central Washington State University)—largely World War II vets—signed a letter protesting Truman's military policies. A major concern was the mounting tension between the West and the former Soviet Union. There was a real fear that the Cold War might develop into World

War III. We did not feel Truman was engaged in a vigorous diplomatic effort to reduce tension between the West and our former Soviet allies. Of additional concern was the giving of aid to the British and French in their attempts to regain control over their crumbling empires. We were particularly outraged by U.S. intervention in Greece's internal affairs. During World War II, the Greeks had mounted a particularly courageous and effective popular insurgency against the occupation of Greece by Nazi Germany. The leadership of this insurgency was largely of the left and intent on shaping post-war Greece into a much more egalitarian society. This was not acceptable to the British. With American aid, the British were intent on imposing on the Greek people the old monarchy and corrupt pre-war system. The result was the disastrous civil war of 1947-1949, from which the Greeks never really recovered. Such events set the tone of our post–World War II atmosphere.

I also have to mention Vietnam. The Vietnamese are a very proud people. From the very first they resisted French occupation and control of their country, as they always had resisted, by one means or another, attempts by outsiders to gain control of their country. During World War II, the Japanese overran Vietnam, and the Vietnamese did what they always did—they resisted. Under the popular leadership of Ho Chi Minh, they put up an extremely courageous and effective resistance, and by the end of WWII controlled large sections of the country. With the defeat of Japan, the French, with American aid and support, attempted to regain control, with disastrous consequences for all three nations—French, American and Vietnamese.

I almost omitted mention of the Chinese resistance to Japanese invaders, both before and during World War II. During the war, we backed Chang Kai-shek and his Kuomintang Party. The fact is, Chang Kai-shek and his Kuomintang Party were hopelessly corrupt and ineffective in their resistance to the Japanese invaders. Our military commander in China during most of World War II was Joseph "Vinegar" Stilwell. Stilwell was a no-nonsense general with an excellent knowledge of Chinese history and culture. Stilwell minced no words in his utter disdain for Chang Kai-shek and the Kuomintang. Instead, he had the greatest respect for the communist fighters under the leadership of Mao Tse-tung. In the end, Stilwell was sacked because of his disagreements with Chang Kai-shek, and Chang's undue influence in Washington, D.C. The unfortunate case about China, as in so many other examples, was that really capable and knowledgeable people were eliminated when most needed.

From the end of World War II on, the United States has followed a policy of suppressing popular insurgencies where, in one form or another, they might be deemed a threat to U.S. power and influence. I reached that conclusion about the overall policy of the United States Government about 40 or 50 years ago. However, it was only recently that I ran across an official statement that that was the case. Below is the "smoking gun," authored by George Kennan, Head of the Policy Planning Staff of the United States State Department, in 1948:

> We have about 50 percent of the world's wealth, but only 6.3 percent of the world's population. In this situation, we cannot fail to be the object of envy and resentment. Our task in the coming period is to devise a pattern of relationships which will permit us to maintain this position of disparity without detriment to our national security. To do so, we will have to dispense with all sentimentality and daydreaming; and our attention will have to be concentrated everywhere on our immediate national objectives. We need not deceive ourselves that we can afford today the luxury of altruism and world benefaction…We should cease to talk about vague and—for the Far East—unreal objectives such as human rights, the raising of living standards, and democratization."

I have given only three examples of the long list of operations carried out by U.S. forces to undermine popular insurgencies or attempts to establish fledgling democracies over the past 70 years. I need also say, in 1948, many of us WWII vets were much disturbed by the reorganization of the military under a single command structure called the "Defense Department." We felt the old term, War Department, was much more accurate. Worse yet, why was an integrated military structure reminiscent of that of defeated Nazi Germany being imposed on us? We didn't understand to any extent the far-reaching changes that were taking place in our country, in both foreign and domestic policy.

NINETEEN FORTY-EIGHT WAS INDEED A MONUMENTAL YEAR.
The "experts" believed the country was tired of Democratic rule, and the Republican candidate, Thomas Dewey, would easily be elected president, for among other things, the Democratic Party was undergoing a three-

way split. Truman held the support of the party regulars, but a significant portion of the ultra-conservative Southern Democrats under the leadership of Strom Thurman of Georgia broke away and formed the Dixiecrat Party, complete with Confederate Flags and symbols including those of the KKK. The Dixiecrats did manage to score some 38 votes in the Electoral College.

Often overlooked in mainstream accounts was the revolt by the more militant New Deal elements. They coalesced under the leadership of former Vice President Henry A. Wallace and formed the "Progressive Party." The Progressives were essentially a popular front of left-wing elements, including communists, but for the most part, the Progressive Party was composed of widely divergent elements containing the spirit of dissent which marked the New Deal period. Progressives were disenchanted with Truman's foreign and domestic policies. Domestically, they felt Truman had not pushed efforts to extend and expand New Deal policies hard enough, and, in particular, had given credence to the ultra-right by caving in to their anti-communist hysteria and red-baiting by instituting loyalty oaths for governmental employees. Opposition to Truman's foreign policy was essential, as I previously indicated by the letter of protest 22 of us students signed and sent off to the White House.

In the end, Dewey was over confident, lacked the dynamism of Truman in his campaigning, and lost the election. But there was an additional element that none of us young people were aware of at the time that added to Truman's victory. The Pro-Israel Zionist element had significant sums of money at their disposal, and were willing to turn some over to Truman's election campaign, should he give recognition to the establishment of a State of Israel on Palestinian soil. Truman indicated such support, and legend has it he received a trunk full of campaign funds with which he financed a nationwide campaign tour by train.

Whatever the truth of the matter, or actual details, we know that Truman gave support to the Zionist cause against the advice of all those persons close to him knowledgeable on Middle Eastern affairs. They included Director of State Department Planning George Kennan, Secretary of Defense James Forrestal, and Secretary of State George C. Marshall. Marshall, in particular, was furious with Truman and resigned along with a good share of the people most knowledgeable on Middle Eastern affairs.

Most of the people in the United States, including us activists at Central Washington State, hailed Truman's action as a great act of contrition toward the long-suffering Jews, and there was a particular satisfaction in providing a homeland for Holocaust survivors. We were totally ignorant of the 1917 Balfour Declaration, which opened up Palestinian territory for land purchases at a time when about 95 percent of the Palestinian population was Muslim or Christian. And even in 1947, about 70 percent of the population was Muslim or Christian, with Jews constituting only about 30 percent. We also never gave a thought to the fact that the Holocaust was a European, rather than a Palestinian, problem.

It was only years later that I began to understand the nature of the tragedy that had been inflicted upon the Palestinian people. They, like most of the Middle Eastern Arabs at the end of WWII, looked to us Americans to help right the wrongs inflicted upon them by the British and French after World War I, when these two nations divided up the spoils of war. Americans, as supporters of the "Right of Self Determination of Peoples," were seen in a very favorable light. All for the sake of a pot of campaign funds and the securing of some tightly knit votes, those hopes of the Palestinian people were dashed to ground, and we Americans earned the lasting hostility of a vast segment of the Arab peoples.

I don't think I can emphasize enough the breach that took place in foreign policy between the Roosevelt and Truman years. The system of patient and careful negotiations with the Russians was gone. Truman once said, "I may not get 100 percent of what I want from Stalin, but I will get 85 percent." Any agreements with the leaders of the former Soviet Union would be on our terms, not theirs. The counter-productive nature of this policy was best stated by Henry Wallace in September 1946: "Getting tough never brought anything real and lasting, whether for schoolyard bullies or world powers. The tougher we get, the tougher the Russians will get." This statement pretty well summarizes U.S.–Russian relations for the past 70 years.

I COMPLETED MY B.A. DEGREE IN SOCIAL SCIENCE at Central Washington State in March, 1949. I was scheduled to enter the History Department of the University of Washington in Seattle at the graduate level in the fall of 1949. However, in the meantime, I had a few problems to solve. I had impacted wisdom teeth to be taken care of, and I was to be married in August, but I had no money. I needed a job badly.

As a teenager, my father had vividly impressed upon me the need to hustle up a job—to hit the road, to stay on it until I found something. So at the end of March, 1949, I hit the road and thought, as in the summer of 1946, it would be a simple matter to find a high-paying construction job and pile up a tidy little sum of money to take care of my new wife and myself until she received her first check from a teaching job she was to start in September.

Sadly, my contacts in the building trades seemed to have dried up, and not much was going on. So, a bit downcast, I headed for the unemployment office, which at that time was located in the Old Armory Building in downtown Seattle. When I arrived, I found the place jammed full of unemployed people looking for work. I couldn't even get in the front doorway. The first post-WWII recession was on. While studying in college, I had little knowledge of the economic changes that were taking place.

It wasn't easy, but I finally qualified for a job on a survey crew with Seattle City Light, way up in the North Cascades on the Skagit River. Even then, I got the job largely due to the fact that I was given extra points on the civil service examination that formed the basis of employment as a result of my WWII service. A new reality was sinking in.

THE RECESSION OF 1949 WAS SHORT, due at least in part to the perceived immediacy of the threat of Soviet power. The perception was fed by the fact that China had fallen to the communist insurgency led by Mao Tse Tung. The right-wingers charged that the loss of China to the communists was due to the weakness of Truman's policies. Truman responded with a vigorous denial and a request to Congress for a substantial increase in military expenditures. Congress promptly complied.

China's loss to Mao Tse Tung's communists was quickly followed by the Korean War of 1950-1953. At the end of WWII, there was some doubt on the part of American leaders as to what was to become of Korea, which had been an integral part of the Japanese Empire during the war. In the end, the Truman Administration decided to occupy South Korea and install a puppet government under the leadership of Dr. Syngman Rhee, a Korean exile living in the United States. As South Korea's head of state, Rhee promptly set up a right-wing dictatorship composed primarily of the same system of administration and control that had served the Japanese so well. Rhee's regime essentially was one of landlords, oligarchs, and police.

Rhee indicated he was militantly committed to liberating North Korea from communist control. Communist North Korea, under the leadership of Kim Il-Sung, was equally committed to liberating South Korea. The result was fighting, which began on June 24, 1950. Exactly who attacked whom first and was responsible for the war was never completely clear. At any rate, the United States, under Truman's leadership, entered the fray on June 25, 1950, with dubious legality, under the guise of a "police action." Ironically, my four-year naval reserve enlistment expired on June 21, 1950, a few days before enlistments were frozen. I was never called back, much to my great relief.

The Korean War would drag on for 37 months with about 36,000 U.S. dead and another 100,000 wounded. The number of Koreans killed or wounded perhaps ran into the millions.

I am tempted to engage in a discussion of the arrogance and ineptitude of our Supreme Military Commander, General Douglas MacArthur. A few remarks are in order. He finally disobeyed the orders of his Commander-in-Chief, President Harry Truman, and was fired. MacArthur returned to the United States as the Great Hero and Darling of the ultra-right. He was wined and dined and paraded. His most famous words were, "Old soldiers never die. They just fade away." At his ticker-tape parade in New York City, an ex G.I. held up a sign that said, "Fade Away." That sign reflected the view of many WWII vets, particularly of the Navy and Marine Corps, who thoroughly detested the man. Some even felt that sacking MacArthur was the greatest thing Harry Truman ever did as President of the United States.

IN MANY RESPECTS, 1952 MEANT A RETURN to politics as usual in this country. The Progressives had faded away, and it was back to two parties—the Democrats and the Republicans. Truman chose not to run again, even though he was eligible. He had served most of Roosevelt's fourth term, plus his own, which meant that he had served nearly two full terms, and would step down in accordance with the two-term tradition of the American Presidency. The real reason for his lack of ardor was the great unpopularity of the Korean War, which dragged on, with no end in sight.

The election of 1952 saw the Democrats run Adlai E. Stevenson of Illinois against World War II hero General Dwight D. Eisenhower, on the

Republican ticket. Eisenhower was a political moderate with no clear political orientation, and at first there was a question as to whether he would run as a Democrat or a Republican. He chose the latter and was elected in a landslide victory, placing the Republicans back in the White House for the first time in 20 years.

The Eisenhower Administration made no big changes domestically. The economy was booming and the "Golden Age" of capitalism was in full swing. Eisenhower did achieve one great thing. In July 1953, a few months after taking office, he brought the Korean War to a close. After 37 months of fighting, a truce was arranged with the demarcation line at the 38th parallel, very near where it was when the fighting began. In essence, the war had accomplished nothing other than solidifying the boundary between North and South Korea. Harry Truman responded to the agreements by saying that had he been willing to accept those terms, he could have ended the war a year earlier, the inference being that Eisenhower was soft on communism.

The Eisenhower Administration was anything but soft on communism. Foreign policy under the leadership of John Foster Dulles was vigorously anti-communist. Any popular movement that in any way could be deigned to have some communist influence was promptly destroyed and an acceptable right-wing government installed.

IT'S IMPOSSIBLE TO WRITE DOWN HERE the whole litany of foreign interventions that took place during the Eisenhower years, which were much in keeping with the imperial grandeur of post–World War II America, but I shall mention two—the 1953 intervention into Prime Minister Mossadegh's Iran, and the 1954 tragic overthrow of Guatemalan President Jacobo Árbenz Guzmán.

Mossadegh's Iran was making slow but steady progress toward becoming a genuine democracy. Mossadegh himself was a rather conservative premier, but he made one fatal mistake. The British controlled the very profitable oil industry. Mossadegh felt that Iranian oil should belong to the Iranian people, and set about nationalizing the oil industry. To the British, this would not do. They promptly got together with appropriate persons in the United States Government—the CIA, of course—and overthrew the Mossadegh regime. The reactionary Pahlevi Regime was promptly installed, ensuring shared control of the oil industry by the British and the Americans. This was not the end, but the beginning of a sequel that haunts us down to the present day.

The second example of the fundamental hostility of the Eisenhower Administration to genuine democracy is the destruction of the government of Jacobo Árbenz Guzmán in Guatemala in 1954. After Guatemala's popular revolution in 1944, the new democratic government set about on a pattern of land reform which meant breaking up control of the land by a few powerful families and foreign corporations and redistributing it to peasant farmers. By 1954, about 100,000 poor peasant families had benefitted. Most of the lands appropriated were idle and paid for on the basis of tax assessments.

In 1954, President Árbenz began extending the land reform. The most extensive unused lands were those of the United Fruit Corporation. Of its great holdings, extending from coast to coast, only about 8 percent were in use. United Fruit, a U.S. corporation, took a jaundiced view of Árbenz's efforts to redistribute some of its unused lands to poor peasants, and promptly sought help from a legal consultant, U.S. Secretary of State John Foster Dulles. John Foster promptly got together with his brother, CIA Chief Allen Dulles. The two brothers arranged to have Colonel Rodolfo Armas, a graduate of the Fort Leavenworth Kansas Military School, to be flown on a U.S. military plane along with a substantial military force to Guatemala, to overthrow the Árbenz government. The result has been lasting disorder in Guatemala and the slaughter of tens of thousands of people, many of them indigenous.

To these examples, we probably should add Vietnam and virtually the entire Middle East. The list is seemingly endless.

The Eisenhower years really represent the early years of the "Golden Age of Capitalism." If we omit the petty little military wars and operations, It was a peacetime economy. The Korean War was over and military expenditures actually declined a bit before beginning to rise toward the end of the Eisenhower period. Under the leadership of Charles Edwin Wilson, former CEO of General Motors Corporation, the Defense Department was reorganized and kept under close civilian control. Charles E. Wilson of General Motors Corporation should not be confused with Charles Edward Wilson of General Electric, famous for implying we were on a permanent war economy, which we were, despite the small reduction in military expenditures. In a sense, the Eisenhower years were the years of the generals—General Eisenhower of WWII fame, Charles E. Wilson of General Motors, and Charles E. Wilson of General Electric.

DOMESTICALLY, THE EISENHOWER YEARS represent the full flowering of the corporate, consumerist economy. Charles E. Wilson of General Motors had a great influence on the Eisenhower Administration that went far beyond the Defense Department. A massive interstate highway program was undertaken, which greatly stimulated the economy and overall prosperity. General Motors Corporation prospered greatly through the sale of high-powered, oversized vehicles, which, toward the end of the fifties, spouted fins. Charles E. Wilson is reputed to have said, "What is good for General Motors is good for the country." What he actually said was "...what was good for the country was good for General Motors." Critics of Eisenhower and Wilson popularized the first version, which was taken as a description of the nature of the Eisenhower Administration.

Now I hate to boast, but I was a fan of neither Eisenhower nor Wilson. I bought Studebakers, made by the Studebaker Corporation in South Bend, Indiana. The Studebaker Corporation was founded in 1851 to make Conestoga wagons for the westward movement. One hundred years later, my wife and I picked up a wonderful little Starlight Coupe at the factory, which we truly loved. My contention has always been that the efficient little Studebakers were far too good for a senseless, wasteful public. GM's high-powered sales pitch blanketing the media, especially TV, put Studebaker and the remaining small auto firms out of business.

On the positive side, corporate profits from a growing economy during the Eisenhower years were pretty much shared across the population. The United States had no real foreign competitors yet, for the economies of Germany, Japan, and other devastated countries were still in process of being rebuilt. American corporations, of course, were investing heavily in these countries. People generally were not aware of the tightening grip large corporations had over them. People were just too busy buying up all the abundant new goods produced by the expanding economy to pay much attention to anything else.

The World War II generation was very busy producing a new generation—the Boomers. Large post-war families demanded large houses, and the housing boom sprouted all sorts of new developments across the country. My wife and I and our family lived in two of them—the first a rather small house, the second a considerably larger house in keeping with a family growing both numerically and age wise. A close friend of mine, kind of a surrogate dad, called the latter development a kid farm.

The "evil eye" soon appeared on the scene to break the tranquility of our lives. The "evil eye," of course, was commercial television. When the TV set appeared after WWII, it was referred to, quite rightly, as "the idiot box." A close friend of mine had an elderly aunt who was mentally challenged, functioning perhaps at a seven- or eight-year-old level. She had been a continual problem for the family, until the advent of TV. After that, she kept herself busy watching television, and that pretty well solved the problem. We were the last house on the block to get a TV set. I only agreed to buy one to get the kids home, so we could control their watching habits to some extent. However, our efforts were largely in vain. With the advent of television, the dumbing-down of America took a gigantic leap forward.

In considering the full flowering of consumerism during the Eisenhower years, we need to back track a bit and take a look at what was going on during World War II. World War II has been called "the total war." Everybody and everything was drafted into the war effort, they said. But the fact is, they were not. The war was never "total." The head of the War Production Board, Donald M. Nelson, was the former head of Sears Roebuck Corporation, one of the nation's largest consumerist firms. Nelson insisted that some part of the nation's economic apparatus should be set aside to provide consumer goods, and it was. Nylon stockings were in short supply, but available, and how the ladies fought over them. The same was true of shirts, blouses, and unmentionables. Good shirts, suits, and ties were still available on a limited scale for men. America really was Number One. We had both guns and butter. One last note: A high ranking Russian official bitterly complained the United States fought the war with American machines, American money, and Russian blood.

AT HIS POINT, I CAN'T HELP BUT CONTRAST Eisenhower's attitude with that of General George C. Marshall. Eisenhower, quite rightly, is given credit for the successful landing on the beaches of Normandy. But Eisenhower was one of George C. Marshall's protégés. It was Marshall who was responsible for the military planning during World War II, and much of that success must be attributed to him.

Marshall was an austere, highly disciplined individual who did not have the relaxed exterior appearance of Eisenhower. Marshall insisted on the strict separation of the military from elected, governmental office. He even refused to vote in elections, with one exception. That exception was when, as Secretary of State, it became apparent that Truman might recognize the State of Israel. Marshall said, in effect, "If you recognize Israel, I will have to vote against you." True, Marshall did serve, post World War II, in a number of high-ranking governmental positions, and the "Marshall Plan" is given much of the credit for the economic, social, and political recovery after World War II, but Marshall's service was always the result of a call from the civilian sector, and not as a result of personal, political ambition.

President Eisenhower's administration was pretty much a relaxed, easy-going affair. To a large extent, he left the actual running of affairs of state to his underlings—people like John Foster Dulles and Charles E. Wilson. Eisenhower did experience a heart attack while in office, from which he never really recovered. One close associate of mine likened the post-attack appearance of Eisenhower to that of a chicken embryo. I felt that was a bit overdoing it. He was robust enough to get out and play golf. We have one thing to thank Eisenhower for, though it came a bit late, and that was his warning about the rising influence of the military-industrial complex. That complex had further consolidated its control during Eisenhower's eight years as president. Under the pressure of the Cold War, it continued to consolidate its control and power over every segment of American society and constituted a real threat to American democracy.

PARTICULARLY TROUBLESOME WERE THE INSURRECTIONS that kept cropping up against right-wing regimes that owed their existence, at least in part, to American support and aid. The Cuban Revolution of 1958, which resulted in Fidel Castro and compatriots taking power on January 1, 1959, certainly was one of the greatest of those events. The impact of the Cuban Revolution continues on down to the present time. In a real sense, the Cuban Revolution dealt a real blow to American power and prestige.

I am tempted to go into considerable detail about Cuban-American relations between 1959 and the reconciliation in 2015, but neither time nor space will permit it. I will make one digression, to discuss the Cuban missile crisis, which I consider one of the least understood events of the 1960s. The Russians brought in a substantial shipload or loads of missiles, and planted them in an open, not camouflaged, area where they were quickly spotted by the ever-alert intelligence apparatus of the

United States. The resulting crisis seemed to put the planet on the verge of a nuclear meltdown. As a result of negotiations, the Russians were forced posthaste to withdraw the missiles. Seemingly, we had won and the Russians had lost.

But had they? In the end, the security of Cuba was guaranteed and there were no more overt military adventures sponsored by the U.S. like the Bay of Pigs invasion. Furthermore, the U.S. withdrew missiles that were threatening Russia from bases in Turkey. Thus, the Russians gained a degree of security, which they very much desired. This part of the story has been almost completely suppressed in the United States.

I would dearly love to discuss the Cuban Revolution in detail, and the example it has set for other suppressed peoples in the Western Hemisphere and on the planet, but detailed analyses of the dynamics of revolution is beyond the scope of this paper. I shall limit myself to a few additional remarks. The leaders of the Revolution were old enough, roughly 25 to 40 years, to have had some unsuccessful revolutionary activism, and therefore some conception of the nature and difficulties they were to encounter, but young enough to have the youthful vitality necessary for such an operation. They also were well educated, but had experienced the frustration of trying to make socially productive use of that education. Finally, they clearly recognized the pain and suffering of the masses, the struggles of peasants and working-class people just to exist in a land governed by a small, wealthy, highly privileged elite backed by the overwhelming force and influence of a foreign imperial power. The people who made the Cuban Revolution had a fairly clear conception of what needed to be done if the effort was to succeed, and they succeeded due to their persistence, imagination, and strength of character.

THE 1950S MARKED QUITE A TURNING POINT IN MY LIFE. I began my teaching career in 1950 in a junior high school in Vancouver, Washington. After six years, I would move up to high school, due to the fact that I was tied to the "Boomer Generation" as they matured. In the fall of 1950, I was still insecure as to my future, not just because I was a beginning teacher, but feeling anxious, lest I be drafted into the Korean War. Fortunately, the war passed me by, and I was able to relax and become completely involved in my new career.

Life always has its complications. In 1952 our first child was born a little ahead of schedule. We found ourselves faced with a single income—mine. Teachers low down on the pay schedule, as I was, were not paid a living wage with regard to being able to support a family. Furthermore, we were paid in ten installments, which meant there were two months when we were without a check. To face this situation, I resorted to past behavior—I set out to hustle up a summer job.

I had an asset without which I might have been in deep trouble. That asset was the Central Labor Council of Clark, Skamania, and East Klickitat Counties. When I entered the teaching profession, I found it was organized in associations that included management—principals and even higher administration. This arrangement smacked to me of company unionism, which, as a product of the North Woods and most particularly of the Seattle area, I found abhorrent.

Consequently, I did something that I felt was perfectly natural. I got together with some other young family men and a few older teachers and set about organizing a genuine union—with free and open collective bargaining as the objective. Our superiors had always proclaimed that teaching was a profession, and above the conditions which led ordinary working people to organize unions. To me, this was nonsense—nothing but company propaganda. We didn't charge fees like doctors and lawyers. We were working for wages, which meant we were working-class like everyone else. And so it was I became heavily involved in the struggle for collective bargaining rights for public employees, and thereby acquired and retained labor affiliation that has lasted down to the present day.

Through my acquaintance with some of the key figures in the local central labor council, I obtained a permit to work through the local building trades. In June of 1952, as soon as I checked out of school, I headed for the hiring hall in downtown Vancouver with my good friend and colleague, Earl Cooke. (Earl's wife was pregnant.) We were fortunate that afternoon, for few people were looking for work. We were there only a few minutes when a call went out for vibrator operators on concrete pours at the Yale Dam Project on the North Fork of the Lewis River, just north of Vancouver. Even though we knew nothing of vibrators, we immediately answered the call, took the appropriate papers, and headed north up the Lewis River. By watching others, we quickly learned to operate the vibrators and a whole lot of other pneumatic tools.

Being out of shape for hard physical work, we did well until our lunch break. Time was called, and everyone sat down with his lunch bucket and began to eat except Earl and I. Earl looked at me, grinned, took out a package of cigarettes and offered me one. (We were both smokers then.) One of the workers looked at us and asked, "Ain't you fellows got any lunches?" We answered that we had to leave for the job in such a hurry we had no time to pick up any food. I have never seen so much food appear in such a short period of time, more than we could possibly handle—a perfect example of worker compassion and solidarity.

We were employed by Morrison/Knudsen Company on the swing shift. Since there was no graveyard concrete crew, we often worked overtime. The pay was great—far more than I earned teaching school. Despite the heavy physical demands, I really enjoyed the work, and especially the camaraderie of working stiffs on a good union job (lots of laughs as well as aching muscles and bones).

At the end of summer, when I was about to quit and go back to teaching school, I was given this advice by one of my friends, a concrete finisher: "Quit teaching. You'll never make any money that way. Stick with me. I'll make a good finisher out of you. Work 30 years for M&K [Morrison/Knudsen], and you can retire with a good pension." Our conversation continued a bit longer. M&K had a contract building a huge airbase at Thule, in Greenland. I was told I probably would make three or four times—a conservative estimate—what I could expect to make teaching school. There were amenities that came with the job, including furloughs for home visitations. This was a lesson on what Cold War military contracting was all about. There were inconveniences, such as weird, isolated places in which to work, but the financial rewards were far beyond what could be expected from regular employment in the states. What was going on in Greenland was a very small matter compared to what would later take place in such places as Vietnam and Afghanistan.

I ignored my friend's advice and returned to teaching, supplementing my meager income by doing heavy construction work during the summers for a number of years. This illustrates, to a considerable degree, the values generally accepted by Americans. Verbally, Americans seem to place a high value on education, but do they really? If one went by the monetary rewards, especially compared to how much is spent to sustain the world's most powerful military, the answer would have to be no. This became particularly apparent when I came into contact with educators in school systems abroad. In other European countries such as Finland, for example, teaching was one of the most sought after and best-rewarded professions. I have often thought of Ancient China where teaching and learning were at the top of the social hierarchy and the military was at the bottom.

What kept me in teaching despite the profession's comparatively meager wages was the chance to continue my education virtually forever, and the wonderful colleagues with whom I had a chance to associate. Most importantly, I had a chance to impart at least some small amount of the knowledge and experience that I had gained to young people. The challenges one faced were continuous, and often of an unforeseen and intense variety, and this added a matchless richness to one's life.

I left the Vancouver School District after six years with a very fine recommendation, and was hired by the Portland Public Schools in almost record time. My theory about the recommendation was that I really didn't merit it. It was a good way of getting rid of me without encumbering additional difficulties.

OVER MY LIFE, I WAS ALWAYS CAUGHT UP in the spirit and life of the times. I didn't like the Kennedys. I can't say exactly why, except the old dad, Joe Kennedy, made a lot of money selling booze and had a rather arrogant, conservative outlook. However, there was a particular glamour about the younger generation, descendants of Irish immigrants, who had risen to the top of the social ladder. Despite the fact that John "Jack" Kennedy's drive for the presidency was vigorously promoted by liberal Democrats who were thoroughly overcome by his handsome appearance and the need to overcome the prejudice against a Catholic at the head of the government, I didn't support him. Yes, along with everyone else on the left, I had fears about what the Evil Richard Nixon might do as president, but I cast them aside and remained somewhat ambiguous about the whole election. Anyway, I always seemed to find someone in a small minority party to support. As it was, Kennedy won, but not by much.

Essentially, Kennedy's short term in office was a continuation of the imperial Cold War course set by the Truman Administration. Besides the Cuban fiascos, there were numerous others. I just can't resist singling one out in particular—the Dominican Republic. In the fall of 1963, Juan Bosch, a popular social democrat who had been elected president by a 60-percent majority of the Dominican people, was overthrown in a military coup blessed by the Kennedy Administration. Examples of popular government were not to be tolerated, particularly when U.S. sugar interests were at stake.

Like most people, I was shocked, perhaps "stunned " is a better word, by the assassination of John F. Kennedy. He was so popular and so much in the limelight. I don't pretend to know who really was responsible, except to say I don't think it was just a single assassin, Lee Harvey Oswald. There were just too many contradictory statements that came out of the official investigation, and too many persons and groups who would benefit by the assassination.

The one thing that sticks out in my mind is the assassination of Oswald by Jack Ruby after Oswald's capture. That was followed by Ruby's mysterious death. Ruby had contacts with the Cuban gambling and crime syndicates, many elements of which had reasons to want Kennedy dead. Even Lyndon Johnson had some doubts about Kennedy's assassination being the act of a single individual.

I HAD HIGH HOPES THAT LYNDON JOHNSON'S ACCESSION to the presidency would mark an improvement in both foreign and domestic policies. Johnson had been an ardent supporter of President Roosevelt's New Deal policies, and had a down-to-earth populist demeanor that connected well with ordinary people. He was an astute politician who understood the workings of Congress and who had the ability to push needed legislation through that body to a successful conclusion. Indeed, in regards to domestic policy, my confidence was well founded. It was under Johnson that important civil rights acts were passed ensuring the rights of African-Americans to vote in southern states. It was also under Johnson that the Civil Rights Movement made important gains in ending racial segregation.

Johnson's Great Society program and War on Poverty made real gains for the common people. It was during this period that the Economic Opportunities Act was passed, which did much to aid poor people. Perhaps most important was the passage of the Medicare Act which guaranteed medical care for older Americans. It was hoped that these benefits would be extended before long to all Americans.

Looking back on the many domestic accomplishments of the Johnson Administration, it seemed as though much of President Roosevelt's Second Bill of Rights would be realized. What was important was that the momentum behind these programs be maintained and if possible, accelerated. Alas, this was not to be.

I voted for Lyndon Johnson for President in 1964. He and Bill Clinton (the first time) were the only two persons I ever voted for that actually won the presidency. My confidence in Johnson was utterly destroyed by the Gulf of Tonkin Incident in 1964 and its consequences—full-fledged warfare in Vietnam. This involvement overshadowed Johnson's domestic achievements, put a damper on its continuation and, in a sense, the war made Johnson one of the most tragic figures in American history.

Initially, Johnson seemed reluctant to increase American involvement in Vietnam, beyond the small number of advisers President Kennedy had already committed to shore up the highly unpopular regime of Ngo Dinh Diem. This South Vietnamese regime had been set up by the United States after the ouster of the French in 1954, as a counter to the popularity of Ho Chi Minh in the North.

Johnson caved in to his advisers and his noisy, vitriolic, right-wing Republican critics by making a commitment to intervene heavily into what had been a Vietnamese war of independence. The intervention was one of the most disastrous in American history, and revealed the basic bankruptcy of U.S. foreign policy. That policy essentially was imperialistic—an attempt to impose U.S. hegemony throughout the globe by maintaining a cadre of client states dependent on U.S. military power for their existence with little regard for the hopes and aspirations of the common people. The inevitable result of U.S. foreign policy has been multiple disasters, with death and destruction spread across much of the planet.

Anti-Vietnam war demonstrations began in the fall of 1965, and I took part in them. I remember the first one, in the spring of 1965, which took place down on Portland's west-side waterfront near the entrance to one of the bridges. There were perhaps 40 or 50 of us, largely World War I and World War II generations. I remember another demonstration, not too much later, when a friend of mine who was old enough to be my dad got very excited. He exclaimed and pointed to some newcomers, "Look at that! Young fellows! Look at the young fellows!" It was the Vietnam generation—no women yet, but they were to follow before long.

I don't think people realize how traditional and ingrained opposition to U.S. imperialism had been in this country. I often think of Mark Twain, and the Anti-Imperialist League, which existed at the end of the nineteenth and turn of the twentieth centuries. Opposition to Wilson and our entrance into World War I was extensive. One estimate put the opposition to U.S. entrance into that war at 80 percent as late as January 1917. I had one cousin threatened by a vigilante group because of his opposition to the war. Disillusionment with the outcomes of World War I was widespread in this country, and there was considerable reluctance to approve President Roosevelt's attempts to give aid and rearm Britain in the face of the threat from Nazi Germany. So in many respects, those of us opposing the war in Vietnam were adding another chapter to the history of war resistance in this country.

THE ACADEMIC YEAR OF 1965-66 SAW ME BACK at the University of Washington completing a master's degree in Russian studies. The work was very demanding, so my ability to participate in anti-war activities was somewhat limited. I remember one early demonstration in the fall of '65 in which possibly 400–500 of us participated. The anti-war movement was growing and the pace was accelerating. I had some contact with the Student Non-violent Coordinating Committee (SNCC) on the UW campus. I felt a little awkward participating in the group, because everyone was on a first-name basis except me. Because of age (39), they called me Mr. Pool.

When I finished my degree in the summer of 1966, I was reassigned to teach Russian and German at Portland's Lincoln High School. The new assignment was very challenging, but I found time to participate with other teachers in anti-war activities. I should also add that most of us were union activists at a time of considerable controversy over the fate of the Portland Public Schools. The years ahead were very busy ones.

I was involved in too many anti–Vietnam War activities to give an accurate account of them, but two demonstrations stand out in my mind. Both took place in San Francisco with tens of thousands of persons. The first I attended with three of my colleagues who were also union activists. The second demonstration I attended with my wife and our four children. The reason I cite these two demonstrations is that they were symptomatic of the growing national anger over the Vietnam War. We protested its brutality, incompetent leadership, and the many lies we were being told. In addition, my wife and I were very concerned over the fate of our eldest son. Fortunately, he didn't have to go. There were many people just like us.

I think the whole Vietnam thing reached a climax with the Kent State Massacre—killing of four persons and wounding of nine more by national guardsmen. No one was ever prosecuted for that heinous crime, but it focused public attention on the war even more intently—its futility, the countless lies we were being told, and the concomitant demoralization of the country.

The Civil Rights Movement and the anti–Vietnam War movement really constituted a single era stretching from about 1960 to the end of the Vietnam War in 1975. These should not be considered separate entities, but rather part of the same movement to establish a more stable, egalitarian, and just society. Certainly Martin Luther King, Jr., saw it that way. Concentration on the war, with its huge expenditures, exacerbated the internal economic and social divisions, and made progress toward that more egalitarian society much more difficult, if not impossible.

The brutality of the crackdown on both civil rights and anti–Vietnam War demonstrators was indicative of the fact that there were important segments of the ruling elite that saw such an upsurge from below as a threat to their power and position. The secret monitoring and harassment of Dr. King by the FBI and J. Edgar Hoover was an indication that there were elements in the power structure that were determined to undermine and break up the movements.

The assassination of Dr. King on April 4, 1968, came as a terrible shock to everyone involved in the civil rights and anti-war movement. As in the case of the assassination of Jack Kennedy, I never bought into the official line of the assassination being the act of a single shooter. There were just too many contradictions in that account. I can't say I have any clear idea as to who was responsible for King's assassination, but I have a deep-seated feeling that they must have been people who had some connection to governmental agencies like the FBI. The assassination of Robert Kennedy later that year also seemed something of a mystery, although I doubt there was any connection between the two events.

THE ADVENT OF RICHARD NIXON in the office of the presidency was to mark a turning point in the civil rights and anti-war era. In a sense, Richard Nixon won the election of 1968 by default. Divisions over the Vietnam War had pushed the Democratic Party into utter disarray, and its candidate, Hubert Humphrey, was to some extent a replay of Lyndon Johnson. Humphrey was a strong New Dealer on domestic issues, but handled the Vietnam War situation in a very wishy-washy fashion. Despite the violent protests at the Democratic National Convention, his stand was not clear. He failed to unite the base of the party behind himself.

Richard Nixon, commonly referred to as "Tricky Dick," set about reinventing himself after his stunning defeat in the 1960 election. He took on a much more relaxed, friendly demeanor. He backed away from the ultra-right red baiting that had been one of his basic characteristics, and began to exhibit more openness. Furthermore, he indicated he would reduce troop levels in Vietnam and eventually bring the war to a close. How he was going to accomplish all this was not clear, but to many people, continuing down the road we were on was not permissible.

It's not my intention here to dwell on the many scandals that afflicted Nixon's reign of deceit and treachery, but I can't help but relate this about the Watergate Scandal. During his testimony regarding this evil affair, my wife would watch his facial expressions intently. All of a sudden she would exclaim, "Right there! He's lying! See! He's lying!" I think she was invariably right. Other than the public humiliation of a forced resignation from office, Nixon escaped the harsh punishment of a criminal. He was pardoned by his successor, Gerald Ford, whom he had appointed to the office of vice president after Spiro Agnew was ousted from office due to malfeasance. If all of this seems crazy, it was within the character of "Tricky Dick."

In foreign affairs, Nixon pretty much followed the Cold War course laid down by Harry Truman. Popular uprisings that might jeopardize the interests of the American corporate state were not to be permitted. A classic example was the ouster of the popular Salvador Allende of Chile in 1973. As an excuse for the U.S. role in this overthrow of a democratically elected president, Nixon's foreign affairs advisor Henry Kissinger said, "We must save the people [Chileans] from themselves."

Nixon's foreign affairs were not completely negative. There was one very positive result, and that was the recognition of the Peoples Republic of China and the opening of diplomatic and trade relations with that country. That action led to a profound change in international relations on a global scale.

Much of Nixon's domestic policy was also very positive and considerably to the left of Democrats Bill Clinton and Barack Obama. Nixon once said, "We're all Keynesians now," in reference to the economics of British economist John Maynard Keynes, who stressed the importance of government taking an active role in economic affairs. Some of the things we should remember Nixon for were the enactment of the Environmental Protection Act, the Occupational Safety and Health Administration, as well as measures regarding public housing, and clean air and water. At one point, Nixon even talked about a basic income for every American family, but dropped that one in a hurry as a result of a furious reaction within his own party.

The Nixon Administration contained key elements that reacted vigorously against the reforms of the 1960s and 1970s, and the popular upsurge that brought them about. Two persons who figured most prominently in this regard were Secretary of the Treasury William Simon, and Lewis F. Powell, Jr., a prominent corporate lawyer and consultant to the tobacco industry. (Nixon later appointed Powell to the Supreme Court.) Powell was most famous for the memo he sent to the U.S. Chamber of Commerce advising members to be more aggressive in protecting the American free-enterprise system from threats on the left that he considered socialistic and communistic. I think Powell was particularly upset by groups like "Nader's Raiders," which were hell-bent on disclosing corporate duplicity and fraud. Ralph Nader was one of the founders of Public Citizen, a consumer advocacy group. Nader later ran for the presidency as an independent. I proudly confess, I voted for him twice.

Businessmen heeded Powell's warning by forming right-wing think tanks like the American Enterprise Institute, American Legislative Exchange Council (ALEC), and most particularly, the Federalist Society. The latter specialized in grooming conservative young lawyers for important positions in government and especially in the judiciary branch. It's important to note that the four most important conservative members of the current Supreme Court—Antonin Scalia, John G. Roberts, Clarence Thomas, and Samuel Alito—have been members of the Federalist Society. These men rendered the critical judgments in the Citizens United case, which in effect undermined campaign finance reform and opened the floodgates for money to flow into the coffers of right-wing groups and their favored candidates for political office. This result has greatly accelerated the drift to the right of our government and society.

But now we must leave the Nixon years and the man we so loved to hate. As a cartoon in *The New Yorker* put it, "See. I told you you would miss him."

IT WAS IN THE 1970S I FIRST BECAME AWARE of the increasing problem of homelessness. I owned a Rambler automobile, which frequently needed repair. I would drop it off at the Rambler dealership—now the site of Powell's Books in Portland—and walk a few blocks up the street to my job at Lincoln High School. One morning I noticed a homeless camp alongside a culvert next to the I-405 Freeway. I knew there were homeless people down on Skid Row, but I had never seen anything like this uptown. That sight was indicative of the fact that the prosperity we had enjoyed in the 1950s and 1960s was coming to an end. We were entering a new era.

Jimmy Carter was elected President in 1976, not because of any program he had—he really had none—but more because of the scandals of the Nixon years. As I recall, his margin of victory was very small, as was voter participation in the election. I didn't vote for Carter simply because, beneath all the vagaries, I detected a drift to the right. I think the Carter years marked a transition internally from the more liberal, humane policies of his predecessors to the hard-nosed neoliberal economic policies of the Regan-Bush period, which essentially determined the direction of policies to be followed by their successors.

Foreign policy was a different matter. It's hard to believe that the present-day Carter, who has so forthrightly championed free and fair elections abroad, followed the imperial policies of his predecessors. Iran, of course, is the classic example. Following the CIA-sponsored coup of 1953 that overthrew the fledgling democracy of Mohammed Mossadegh, the brutal autocracy of Shah Mohammed Reza Pakhlavi was installed, much to the joy of American and British interests. The Iranian people were not content to accept this state of affairs. Iran really was a well-developed country with a layer of highly educated people, some of whom had spent years in the West. By the 1970s, the utter corruption and brutality of the Pakhkavi Regime had alienated a good share of the population. The result was the Revolution of 1979, which overthrew the Shah and ended with the sacking of the U.S. Embassy and the capture and internment of its employees by militant young Iranians, many of whom had a strong orientation toward Islamic fundamentalism. Carter took the Shah under his protection and granted the Shah asylum.

Now interestingly, the Iranian Revolution took Carter and his aids and advisors by surprise, but it was no surprise to me. I had been reading for months about the Iranian revolutionary build up in *The Nation* magazine and other left-wing publications. What was surprising was the utter ignorance and incompetence of the Carter Administration in dealing with the situation in Iran.

The end result of this fiasco was, of course, the Hostage Crisis of

1979-1980, in which American Embassy employees were held as bargaining chips to gain concessions from the United States. By October 1980, it looked as though Carter had struck a bargain with the revolutionists and the hostages would be released, but this was not to be. They were finally released at the end of January 1981, just as Carter was leaving office, on the eve of Ronald Reagan being sworn in as the new President of the United States.

This whole sequence may seem curious. The last thing the Republicans wanted was the resolution of the Hostage Crisis on the eve of the 1980 Presidential Elections. There were reports from a number of sources, including Iranians who were more secular and forced to emigrate later, of a secret meeting between representatives of the Republican Party and those of the Revolutionary Iranian Government. Among the alleged Republican attendees was Bill Casey, who later became CIA director under Ronald Reagan. According to the reports, a deal was struck whereby if the Iranians would hold off releasing the hostages until after the election of 1980, they would get better terms or concessions from the Republicans than from the Democrats. This was what happened. The October Surprise was averted and Ronald Reagan was elected President.

REAGAN FOLLOWED THE WELL-SET Cold War foreign policies of his predecessors with gusto. He ramped up military expenditures and engaged in a series of military adventures very much in keeping with U.S. Imperialist Interests. The most infamous of these adventures is the one referred to as the Iran-Contra Scandal, in which Reagan sold arms to the Iranians in order to finance counter revolutionaries to put down popular movements in Honduras, El Salvador, and Nicaragua. This was done because the misadventure was illegal and Congress would not appropriate funds to finance it.

Central America was one vast sea of petty dictatorships and undemocratic governments supported by the United States. One of the worst was the corrupt Somoza Regime in Nicaragua. Virtually the entire population rebelled in what was called the "Sandinista Revolution." Somoza and his men were expelled. Reagan had no legal authorization to intervene in Nicaragua. To finance the operation, he sold arms to the Iranians and used the money to hire and arm mercenaries who attacked the Nicaraguans from neighboring Honduras, causing extensive death and suffering among the Nicaraguan people. These mercenaries were called "counter revolutionaries" or "Contras."

There were protests here in the U.S. against the nefarious actions by Reagan and his henchmen. The protests were often brutally put down, resulting in injuries to the protestors, including one of our own Veterans For Peace members, S. Brian Willson, who lost his legs in Concord, California, while trying to stop a naval train loaded with arms destined for the Contras.

The Portland Central American Solidarity Committee (PCASC) was organized at this time to aid the Nicaraguans and other peoples of Central America in their struggle for peace and social justice. One Portlander, a brilliant young electrical engineer named Ben Linder, was killed by the Contras while erecting a hydro-electrical plant which would provide electricity to a local village. I was active in PSASC for a time, and had the privilege of getting acquainted with Ben's mother. I think we all understood clearly that the struggle of the peoples of Central America was inseparable from our own.

After several more years of struggle against the harassment and attempted subversion by the United States, the Sandinistas were able to prevail, and today Nicaragua is one of the freest of all the Central American countries. Nicaragua is an excellent illustration of the nefarious nature of Reagan's foreign adventures.

Essentially, Ronald Reagan was a Grade B movie actor. Acting initially was his career and the means by which he became known throughout the country. When television came along, his movie career folded. However, he was fortunate. He obtained a job hosting a General Electric television show. In that way, he maintained his appearance before a mass audience and became a valuable asset to the corporate cabal that was running the country. Through his association with General Electric, he became acquainted with corporate executives who found him to be an ideal instrument in promoting their policies. It was through that association that Reagan entered politics and would exert a decisive influence on the subsequent course of American history.

Reaganomics really meant a return to policies preceding the New Deal, and contained an outright attack on gains made by working people during that time. Social welfare programs came under increasing scrutiny, and limitations were placed on them. Trade unions came under assault, and their decline, which had already begun, was greatly accelerated. Regulation of business activities was reduced, and we entered the era of "neo-liberal" economic policies that has prevailed down to the present. This transition was not smooth; it was marked by protests held widely throughout the country on behalf of poor working people. These protests were symptomatic of more pronounced ones that were to follow and which continue to the present day.

Ronald Reagan transformed the country in other ways. In particular, He stepped up the war on crime and drugs. He promoted the "three strikes and you're out" policy, by which, if a person was convicted of three felonies or more, he was automatically sentenced to life in prison. The prison population soared from about 400,000 persons when he took office to over a million before he left office. His successors followed his policies and eventually the U.S. prison population grew to over two million. The "prison-industrial complex" was booming. Persons of color were disproportionately objects of suspicion, arrest, prosecution, and conviction. In effect, a "New Jim Crow System" was born.

The Reagan-Bush period did have one positive aspect. After a huge military buildup, tensions were relaxed with Russia. With the reunification of Germany, and Russia's plans to withdraw her forces from Eastern Europe, the Russians wanted assurances that there would be no expansion of NATO forces eastward, into Eastern Europe. These assurances were given through George H.W. Bush's Ambassador to Russia, Jack Matlock. It looked as though many of the Cold War problems would be solved.

THE REAGAN-BUSH PERIOD NOT ONLY MARKED a very significant change in our national life, but also in my personal one. In the fall of 1986, completely worn out after 36 years of teaching, I decided to take early retirement. My problems peaked when my program was changed from teaching four sections of Russian and one of German to teaching four sections of Russian and two of American History, a subject I had taught eight years previously. A program switch such as this meant considerable adjustment, not the least of which was the need to develop supplementary teaching materials for the history classes, and I had to give up my preparation period to maintain the integrity of my third- and fourth-year Russian classes. These two classes were one or two students short of the size required to keep them as separate entities. To separate them, I had to agree to give up my preparation period and teach six classes instead of five. The result was overload, with no weekends or evenings free. When I agreed to the program, I forgot I was no longer young.

Now as strange as it may seem, all this brings us back to Russian-U.S. relations. Through the twists and turns of my life, I happened to get into Russian studies and teaching, which took me to Russia and the former Soviet Union eight times on various programs. It took only one such travel experience for me to realize the American perception of the Russians was horribly distorted. That first experience was on a National Defense Education Act (NDEA) travel/study program, which culminated with final exams in Helsinki, Finland. During a brief respite, I remember one of our members remarking," Everything they told us about the place was false." Both at that time and later times, I found upon my return that most people in this country were not interested in my experiences. Their questions were of a more-or-less simplistic, polite nature.

I also ran four study/travel programs, granting joint credit from the Portland Public Schools and Portland State University to my students. Several days after our return to the States, I asked my students about the reactions of their friends and relatives to their Russian experience. Similarly, my students answered that interest was minimal, and it was difficult to impart much of anything that they had experienced to their friends and relatives. One final notation about my experiences with Russians: My reception by them was always warm and hospitable. I only wish I had the capacity to return more of the same.

My last study/travel experience with my students was most fortunate. It took place in the summer of 1986, a year after Mikhail Gorbachev became head of state and the programs of Perestroika (Restructuring) and Glastnost (New Opening) were really getting underway. There was free expression and association not previously experienced in the former Soviet Union. One additional benefit that accrued to us was that our weeklong Russian language seminar did not take place in Leningrad (Now St. Petersburg), with all its sharp traders and artificial environment. Instead, it was in Krasnodar, the center of the Kuban, Southern Russia's rich agricultural region. Almost immediately, my students made friends with young people their own age, thereby benefiting to a degree students of my previous programs had not. I came away that summer with great hopes for mutual understanding and cooperation between Russians and Americans.

WHEN ONE CONSIDERS THE DIFFERENCE between the Russian reality and the American perception of it, one can readily understand how easy it is to ramp up fear of the Russians and use it as a foggy entity behind which huge military expenditures can be made and used as an instrument for advancing U.S. interests abroad. There was a brief period, during the administration of President George H.W. Bush, when it appeared some degree of understanding and mutual self-interest would result in a significant reduction of tension and widespread agreements between Russia and the West. There had been previous negotiations on the matter of arms control with their ups and downs, but what marked this period as different was the change in Russian policy toward Eastern Europe. Under Mikhail Gorbachev's leadership, Russia sought to reduce tensions by reducing military expenditures, thereby creating more resources for reconstruction of the Russian economy and society. With the freeing of Eastern Europe and in particular East Germany from Russian control, the Russians sought assurances that there would be no expansion of NATO eastward. Those assurances were given to the Russians through our very capable, long-time diplomat and Ambassador to Russia, Jack Matlock. For a time it looked as though Eastern Europe would act as a neutral buffer between Russia and the West.

That perception was quickly shattered when Bill Clinton became president in 1993 and U.S. foreign policy again assumed a very aggressive posture. With the dissolution of the former Soviet Union, it appeared the United States had no rival and could assume the position as the guardian of law and order throughout the planet. Secretary of State Madeleine Albright termed the United States "the indispensable nation," and a series of overseas aggressive actions and military adventures took place in rapid succession—including expansion of NATO into Eastern Europe, with an arrogance that showed contempt for previous assurances given to the Russians that this would not occur.

The arrogant aggressiveness of the Clinton Administration's basic performance and attitude did not escape criticism, at home or abroad. Both France and Germany complained of the use of "hyper power" by the U.S., and its lack of sensitivity in its relations with other nations. Most important was the opposition to NATO expansion by the Arms Control Association, which consisted of a group of prominent foreign policy experts including former U.S. senators, retired military officers, diplomats and academicians. It's interesting to consider some of the names: Ambassador Jack Matlock, Senator Mark Hatfield of Oregon, former Defense Secretary Robert McNamara, and academician Paul H. Nitze, among others. The basis of their criticism of Clinton's foreign policy was that it would heighten Russian suspicions and fears of the West, and scuttle any attempt to control nuclear weapons and ballistic missiles through the Start II and III treaties. But Clinton and company paid little attention to these criticisms, and the opportunity was lost for achieving some real understanding and reduction of tension between Russia and the West.

I VOTED FOR BILL CLINTON IN 1992 with the hope that this new generation, young and energetic, would bring new policies to the national scene, regenerating the populist policies of the New Deal and returning to the principles of the Democratic Party that I had known as a boy. Instead, what I found was a rank betrayal of virtually everything I had ever believed in. The Clinton years marked my permanent break with the Democratic Party, left a very bitter taste in my mouth, and made me a mortal enemy of Clintonism and everything it stood for.

Essentially, what Clinton treated us to was Neo-Reaganism. He promised to end welfare as we know it—and he did, with disastrous consequences for millions of poverty-stricken Americans. I think of one single mother who had to give up her college education, and go to work at a minimum wage job, for a reduced income level, and lost all hope for a better future. Clinton made an ill-founded attempt at instituting national health insurance, which discredited the concept for a long time. In keeping with neoliberal economic theories, he shoved through the North American Free Trade Act (NAFTA), which resulted in extensive factory closings and job losses in this country, and was a disaster in Mexico, where about two million Mexican farmers and small business people were put out of work. The result was a flood of Mexican immigrants crossing the border into this country, and a sequence of related problems that we are still trying, in vain, to deal with today. There was also his cozy relationship with the banking industry—most notably Goldman Sachs and Chase Manhattan. The result was the repeal of the Glass-Steagall Act with its regulatory system, which had functioned to separate regular banking from speculative investment banking. The absence of that regulatory system was a major factor contributing to the financial collapse of 2007–2008. For the life of me, I have never been able to get Democrats to admit complicity in this matter.

The Clinton years were not without opposition; by that I mean real opposition from the left. November 29, 1999, was one of the most memorable days in my life, and in the lives of the thousands of Americans who got caught up in a massive protest against Clinton, NAFTA, and the World Trade Organization (WTO). The meeting of leaders of this organization was scheduled to take place in an uptown facility in Seattle, and their opponents from organized labor, environmental, and social and economic justice groups were determined it should not take place. By means of a massive march and blockade of streets, we demonstrators hoped to close access to the meeting. We were not successful in that respect, but did manage to close down much of central Seattle. Much of the blame for the failure of the effort can be placed on the leadership of the AFL-CIO, who weakened and sold out at the last minute, breaking the unity of the movement. The AFL-CIO leadership was simply too closely tied to the Democratic Party and the economic establishment.

Essentially, the Reagan-Bush I/Clinton years are a single period that marked the triumph of neoliberal economic dogma with the concomitant outcome of disparity in wealth and income growth and disposition between the vast mass of people and the small elite at the top of the social, economic, and political pyramid. At the end of World War II, we were the most egalitarian of all Western Nations. Now, we are the least. Basically, the Democratic and Republican Parties are a set of Siamese twins. They may look somewhat different at the top, but are joined together at the base. We ordinary Americans must give up any illusion that meaningful change toward a more egalitarian, just society will ever come from the top, within that system. Meaningful change must come below, outside the system, erupting spontaneously like the Occupy Movement.

I AM TEMPTED TO ELABORATE IN DETAIL about the sins of the Clinton Administration, but I will restrict myself to one final remark, concerning the "War on Drugs." Here we have a remarkable continuity from the Nixon years on. The War on Drugs was begun by Richard Nixon and continued on through Carter, Reagan, Bush I, and Clinton Administrations, and down to the present time, where finally some effort is being made to counteract its effects, if not bring it to an end. As mentioned before, when Reagan came into office, about 400,000 persons, disproportionately persons of color, were incarcerated in state and federal prisons, and the rate of incarceration was increasing rapidly, particularly since Reagan found it a very useful political tool.

The mass incarceration of persons disproportionately of color was indicative of the deep divisions that were developing in our society. While the rate of incarceration of African-Americans, largely males, has always been somewhat larger than that of Americans of European extraction, the differences had never been particularly large. One only has to take a look at President Roosevelt's Second Bill of Rights to see that there was a real intention to end discrimination in terms of race, religion, and gender. At the 1944 Democratic National Convention, Vice President Henry Wallace said point blank, "There must be no inferior races." What was taking place from the Nixon years on was the development of "A New Jim Crow System." It wasn't just the War on Drugs, but the switch to neoliberal economic policies that accentuated a series of divisions in society. African-American males had always been the "last to be hired" and the "first to be fired." Gains made by African-Americans during World War II and the immediate post-war years were being erased, despite significant gains made by the Civil Rights Movement.

To me, Bill Clinton's decision not just to ride along on the War on Drugs but to accelerate it, thus adding to the system of mass incarceration, was one more indication of his departure from the very basic values of the New Deal Democratic Party, which had made it so great. He lacked the will or capacity to wage an all-out fight for basic elements of economic and social justice. To me, the Clinton Administration marked the slippery slide down a slope into a moral abyss which was to characterize the Bush II and Obama Administrations that followed.

The 1990s were unique in that the United States, with the dissolution of the former Soviet Union, emerged as the world's sole super power. In the words of Frances Fukuyama, former Reagan State Department official, it was the "end of history." Essentially, it was the ultimate triumph of corporate capitalism and the neoliberal economic model it represented. It was the triumph of "American Exceptionalism." The dominant corporate, consumerist culture would prevail everywhere throughout the planet.

NOW, WE NEED TO PAUSE and take a look at what really happened to the former Soviet Union. The common answer given by corporate media is that it "imploded," with no further explanation as to what that term meant. Please note, I used the term "dissolution," which I think is a more accurate rendition of what actually took place. The former Soviet Union had a constitution, but with the rapid changes taking place in the region 1989–1999, it was obvious it needed revising. By August 1991, nine of the Soviet republics, including Russia, Belarus, and the Ukraine, had more or less worked out a system for revision of the constitution that would allow for more autonomy to each of the republics. About 80 percent of the population of the former Soviet Union favored keeping the Union in tact, in revised form.

However, in December 1991, the heads of the three Slavic states—Russia's Boris Yelsin, the Ukraine's Leonid Kravchuk, and Belarus' Stanislav Shushkevich—gathered together in secret at Belovezh, a hunting lodge located on the Belarus-Polish border. There they drafted a document dissolving the former Soviet Union and declaring its members to be independent states. Their action was unconstitutional and considered by many, including the British Ambassador, to constitute a coup d' etat. I think it is most accurate to say the Soviet Union was dissolved by a coup.

The reason for the selection of the hunting lodge on the Belarus-Polish border by the three participants—Yelsin, Kravchuk, and Shushkevich—was the fear that, if their plans were found out prematurely, they might be caught and tried for treason, a crime that, if tried and found guilty, carried the death penalty. To avoid that outcome, they could easily escape across the Polish border. It has been reported that upon completing the nefarious scheme, the participants celebrated in good old Russo-Ukrainian fashion by getting uproariously drunk.

One last remark about what happened to Russia in the 1990s: Boris Yeltsin called in the Harvard Boys—Larry Summers and Jeffrey Sachs, among others—to advise him on how to convert Russia to a free-market economy. The advice he received was, "Shock Treatment," via rapid conversion to the free market. Although they recognized there might be serious consequences, the theory was that there would be a rapid recovery. What happened was a free fall in the Gross Domestic Product (GDP) to about 50 percent of its former self. (Some experts put the figure at 80 percent.) The result was a complete disruption of Russian society. Recovery only came later, under Vladimir Putin's leadership. He definitely turned his back on American advisors and influence. The new phase of Russian-American relations was to be just as critical to world peace as the relations that had existed with the former Soviet Union.

THE ELECTION OF 2000 was one of the most memorable in American history, not just because it marked the beginning of a new millennium, but because the victor, George W. Bush, was a minority president in the sense he had fewer of the popular votes than his democratic rival Al Gore, but won the critical majority in the Electoral College. Most famously, he won the vote in the critical State of Florida. There were all sorts of legal maneuvers that are beyond the scope of my knowledge and imagination, but I will make a couple of remarks. The voter rolls had been purged by Governor Jeb Bush, George's brother, and many voters had erroneously been eliminated from voter eligibility lists which, had they voted, could easily have turned the election the other way in favor of the Democrat Al Gore. Also in Florida, all convicted felons lose the right to vote, which eliminates a great number of people of color— another example of the New Jim Crow.

I didn't vote for Al Gore, Jr., although I had a certain respect for the Gore family, particularly Albert Gore, Sr., who had taken a firm stand against the Vietnam War. Instead, I voted for consumer advocate and populist Ralph Nader on the Green Party ticket. I have voted Green in every election since 1996 except one, primarily because whatever faith I might have had in the ability of the Democratic Party to govern in the interests of ordinary working people was completely shattered by Bill Clinton's eight years in office.

I took an active part in the Nader Campaign of 2000, just as I had in 1996. I remember one huge rally we had at Portland's Rose Garden Arena. Several thousand people took part, and there were lots of little booths around with persons and materials representing environmental and social action groups. I can't remember how many votes Nader got in 2000, but the numbers were fairly large. The Green Party, although still in existence, has largely faded from view since then. No progressive third party can make much of a dent in our political system without very solid labor support. The Blue-Green Alliance we had on November 29, 1999 was very much a passing phenomenon, and quickly evaporated. Organized labor has stuck by the Democratic Party despite the stagnation or loss of income by most Americans, which can only mean a further stagnation or loss of income for the foreseeable future. This development, coupled with the increasing capture of income and wealth by a very small elite at the top of the social and economic pyramid, has made it increasingly unlikely for those at the bottom of the pyramid to wield any real form of political power and influence.

One of the nastiest outcomes of the election of 2000 was that many

Liberal Democrats blamed Ralph Nader and those of us who supported him for Al Gore's loss of the election and the Republican victory. Particularly bad was the fact that through the Bush Presidency, the Republican right wing gained power and influence, enabling them to stack the Supreme Court with ultraconservative judicial appointments.

The fact was that the Gore Campaign lacked real clarity in its program, and was a disorganized mess from the start. Its performance in the Florida election was pitifully naïve and lacked necessary, decisive action. The tragedy of the moribund liberal class is that it has failed to take responsibility for its own deficiencies. Instead, it has taken the easy route by scapegoating others for its failures. I have to add that many of the attacks on Ralph Nader were downright vicious.

ON SEPTEMBER 10, 2001, I HAD A MINOR OPERATION at a Kaiser facility that necessitated an overnight stay in the hospital. Unfortunately, I had a spinal injection for anesthesia that resulted in air getting into my spine. This caused severe pain in the back of my neck, which prevented me from sleeping. About midnight, my roommate, who also could not sleep, turned on the TV for the news. We were both awake on the early morning of September 11, 2001, when the terrorist assault on the World Trade Center took place, and with horror, we watched the sequence of events on television. I think all Americans realized our lives would never be the same after that.

George W. Bush and those close to him took advantage of the situation immediately, and utilized it as an excuse to expand their power and influence domestically and throughout the globe. Initially, the Bush Administration had been a rather lackluster affair without a great deal of public support, but the events of September 11, 2001 changed all that. Just like on December 7, 1941, after the Japanese bombed Pearl Harbor, the people in shock and fear rallied behind their government and demanded revenge for the horrible crimes that had been committed. This degree of support allowed George W. Bush to engage in acts that would have been unthinkable at any other time.

There has been a lot of controversy over Bush's failure to act on intelligence information about the dangers posed by Osama bin Laden and Al-Qaeda. This information was made known as early as the Spring of 2001 by Richard A. Clarke, chief counter-terrorism advisor on the National Security Council. By the summer of 2001, Clarke had information that the country was under the threat of an imminent attack by the Al-Qaeda, and again the information was passed on to senior officials closest to the President. For whatever reason, Bush failed to respond to the warnings. At the 2015 National Convention of Veterans For Peace, the Clarke allegations were confirmed by CIA veteran Ray McGovern.

There are a lot of conspiratorial theories about what actually happened on 9/11/2001, but I don't see any point on spending much time on any of them. However, I do have something of an opinion of my own, based on that intelligence failure coupled with the TV coverage of Bush's reaction upon hearing the news of the 9/11 attacks. He was in Florida, as I recall, reading with children in a school classroom. Upon receiving the news, his face showed no shock or dismay. It was as if he was expecting something of the sort. Perhaps he didn't know exactly what to expect, but his reaction was not what one would normally expect from a person in his position. It seemed to me to be not in accord with that of most Americans. Considering the course Bush and company were to follow in the days, months, and years ahead, I think it very wise to regard all their actions with a high degree of suspicion.

One additional thought keeps bothering me. Fifteen of the 19 terrorists involved in the 9/11 attacks were Saudi citizens. The Bush family has always been close to the Saudis, in part, I think, as a result of their interest in the oil business. Forever imprinted in my mind is the image of President George H. Bush walking hand and hand down a lane with a Saudi Prince—the Saudi Ambassador, I believe. At the time, I couldn't help but wonder, "What the Hell has American Democracy come to, with its President engaging in affectionate relations with the representative of a nation guilty of some of the worst human rights abuses on the planet? What about the beheadings and the oppression of women?"

The military actions of the Bush Administration in Afghanistan and Iraq should not have come as a surprise to anyone who had access to any information beyond the regular commercial media. Among other things, I was getting regular reports on Middle Eastern affairs through both *Monthly Review* and *The Nation* magazines. Most valuable were my personal contacts—friends and acquaintances in the Portland area that had been active in the peace and social justice movements.

IN THE FALL OF 2001, NOT LONG AFTER 9/11, a conference was held at Portland State University on the situation in Afghanistan. Among the things discussed was the fact that one of our large oil companies had been negotiating with the Taliban to bring an oil pipeline from the Soviet Republic of Turkmenistan, through Afghanistan and Pakistan, to the Pakistani Port of Karachi on the Arabian Sea. This development would reduce Western Europe's dependence on oil and gas imports coming through Russia, thus weakening her influence and power. The Afghan War ended that possibility. However, the strategic position and resources of Afghanistan were carefully taken into account as part of the reason for U.S. intervention in Afghanistan.

Most important was information on the presence of the Al Qaeda leader Osama Bin Laden in Afghanistan. According to officials of the Bush Administration, the failure of the Taliban to turn over Bin Laden to the United States to stand trial for war crimes was the reason for war against the Taliban in Afghanistan. However, this is not quite the case. The Taliban offered to give up Bin Laden, provided they could turn him over to a neutral third party. The Bush Administration rejected this offer and went to war. Selling war to the American people was a very easy matter for the Bush Administration. All they had to do was to keep on repeating the words, "Al Qaeda! Osama Bin Laden! Osama! Osama! Osama!" The repetition of a word is a very effective propaganda technique. There were both local and national demonstrations against the war in which I took part, but they had little effect.

I can't help but reflect on information, provided by persons who had been there, about what Afghanistan was like before the U.S. began active intervention in the country. A very good friend of mine and something of a surrogate father, Les Smith, was there for several months in 1948. Les was an agronomist and soil scientist. At that time he was working for Morrison-Knutson Company on an agricultural project to drill water wells and install irrigation works so as to improve the Afghan system of agriculture. Les liked the Afghan people. He found them friendly and hospitable, quite a peaceful sort, unsophisticated and lacking in education. Like many young Westerners, my two sons ventured through Afghanistan in the 1970s on their way to India. Again, the place seemed quite peaceful and hospitable.

I also remember stories about how citizens of Kabul enjoyed films made in India. Afghanistan seemed to be a country traveling at its own pace, adapting to a changing world. We should keep this in mind when we consider what has happened to Afghanistan since the U.S. began active intervention.

THE PRETEXT FOR THE WAR IN IRAQ was quite different from that of Afghanistan. During the eight-year-long Iran-Iraq war, the United States had given aid to Iraq, particularly intelligence information, which in effect made Iraq and Saddam Hussein an ally of the United States. Consequently, some type of story had to be concocted to provide cover for the invasion. The quickest fix seemed to be to link Saddam Hussein to Al Qaeda and 9/11, but since Saddam was an opponent of Al Qaeda, that maneuver was obviously a very poor one. The technique hit upon was to accuse Saddam of harboring weapons of mass destruction—chemical, biological, etc.—and a nuclear weapons development program which threatened the peace and security not just of the United States, but of the entire world. The story was pretty well sold to the American public and the U.S. Congress, which by joint resolution, on October 16, 2002, authorized the use of force against Iraq.

The Weapons of Mass Destruction Story, of course, was false, and the Bush Administration did whatever it could to suppress information to the contrary. The truth of the matter was that, according to the terms of the treaty ending the First Gulf War in 1991, Iraq had to give up all weapons of mass destruction and had no nuclear program worthy of note. This information was given to U.S. authorities through the desertion of Saddam's son-in-law, Lieutenant General Hussein Kamal, in February 2003. Hussein Kamal had been in charge of all nuclear, chemical, and biological weapons. The accusation that Iraq was engaging in a nuclear weapons program was especially spurious, since Mohammed El Baradei, head of the International Atomic Energy Authority, had indicated that was not the case. The Bush Administration engaged in an attempt to discredit El Baradei, but it failed.

The fact that the story invented by the Bush Administration to justify the war against Iraq was fictitious was obvious from the start to a large number of people in this country, and some very large anti-war demonstrations ensued. I took part in one such demonstration in Portland, Oregon, in February 2003. According to some estimates, about 37,000 people participated in that demonstration, which made it one of the largest anti-war demonstrations since the Vietnam War. But the demonstrations had little effect on the Bush Administration. In March 2003, it took the country to war in Iraq—an act that would destabilize the entire Middle East. It's important to note that Congress passed the resolution authorizing the war with only one dissenting vote, that of Representative Barbara Lee of California. Even such notables as Hillary Clinton and John Kerry voted for it.

There has been a lot of discussion of the Iraq War and the spurious reasons the Bush Administration gave for it, but little discussion of the actual reasons for the war other than it had something to do with oil. In a sense, it was a reversal of U.S. policy, since the U.S. had supported Iraq in the eight-year Iraq-Iran War. So what were the real reasons? Some of the information I got indicated the underlying cause of the war was Saddam Hussein's manipulation of the price of oil by controlling the ebb and flow of Iraq's oil on and off the market. By doing so, he was affecting not only the price of oil, but also currency rates—particularly the Euro and the dollar. Such an act, of course, would be an unforgiveable sin.

The United States invasion of Iraq was an unprovoked action in direct violation of the United Nations' Charter and the Universal Declaration of Human Rights. With the invasion and occupation of Iraq, the United States lost whatever moral authority it may have once possessed. With it came the notorious prison camp of Abu Ghraib and the systematic torture of its inmates, including such things as waterboarding, electric shock treatments, and sleep deprivation. One should note that Lane Cotter, former head of the notorious Texas prison system, was hired to run Abu Ghraib.

Prisoners suspected of insurrectional activities often suffered extraordinary rendition to countries noted for their vast array of torture techniques. While detailed discussion of the techniques used at Abu Ghraib is not possible, I feel the need to call attention to one very vital aspect of them. American physicians and psychologists cooperated in developing and perfecting these torture techniques. In this respect, the torture program bore a striking resemblance to that which Nazi Germany employed during World War II.

WE COULD GO ON ENDLESSLY discussing the brutal actions of the Bush Administration, but I will limit myself to just one more—the naval base at Guantánamo Bay, Cuba. In part, it was converted to a prison camp containing inmates, some of whom were later proven innocent of the crimes for which they were accused and incarcerated. Even after years of litigation, they still remained under lock and key. In 2008, Barack Obama promised to quickly close Guantánamo if elected president. Here it is November 2015, and despite Obama's promise, Guantánamo still remains in operation as a prison. The blame for that failure can be placed on the Obama Administration and Congress.

The abuses at Abu Ghraib and Guantánamo were too extensive to be kept secret for long. As they became known, a demand arose both here at home and abroad, that those responsible for such gross human rights abuses should be held accountable. An investigation ensued, the results of which, I think, were perfectly predictable to anyone familiar with the armed forces chain of command. Those at the bottom were forced to face courts martial trials, and when found guilty, were either expelled from the military, or in worst cases, sent to prison. The Abu Ghraib commander was relieved of the command and demoted, while those higher up in the chain of command received reprimands, but little else. At the very top, President Bush, Vice President Cheney, and Defense Secretary Rumsfeld escaped unscathed, with little more than some hue and cry from the regular media. Thorough analysis was largely left to the few independent journalists and commentators, largely on the left, along with a few independent radio and television stations.

The abuses at Abu Ghraib, Guantánamo, and other camps—I should mention Bagram in Afghanistan, since it was one of the worst, established with the U.S. invasion of 2001—certainly were no aberration. Such abuses were abundant during the Vietnam War, and have been seen throughout Central America where much of the military and police forces have been trained at the School of the Americas (now the Western Hemisphere Institute for Security Cooperation) in Fort Benning, Georgia. We shouldn't forget the genocide that took place in Guatemala, or the fact that American military personnel were employed at times with local military units.

But for the moment, let's put the past behind us and concentrate on Bush, Cheney, and Rumsfeld. In the final analysis, they were responsible for the abuses that took place in Afghanistan and Iraq. The problems did not originate at the bottom, with low-level perpetrators of the atrocities, but at the top. It was Bush, Cheney, and Rumsfeld who used their power to initiate the wars, set the machinery in motion to control the populations, and suppress the inevitable opposition. We also need to mention

the extensive suffering and mass casualties among the civilian population. Unlike Vietnam, not much effort has been made by our authorities
to give anything resembling an accurate accounting of civilian casualty
figures, let alone serious discussion of them. The best information I have
as to the number of civilian deaths in the Iraq war is 60,000, a statistic
offered fairly early in the war by the British medical journal, *The Lancet*.
Other organizations, such as the International Red Cross and the United
Nations, gave additional estimates. As the years have passed, it has
become increasingly difficult to give an accurate accounting of casualties
because the death and destruction have become too extensive, along with
the mass displacement of populations.

Essentially, what has happened in the last decade and a half is that the
United States has become embroiled in a morass from which it cannot
apparently extricate itself. There is no end in sight. The objective of our
military strategies supposedly has been to keep our nation safe, but even
though we spend as much money on our military as the rest of the world
combined, the policy of military supremacy has not only not made us
safer, but has had the opposite effect. Somehow, the American people
have not caught on to the fact that the policies promulgated by their
leaders are not just ineffective, but fundamentally wrong.

With the Vietnam War, it became apparent the country had lost its
moral compass and no longer had the credibility to pass itself off as
the number-one proponent of human rights and justice throughout the
world. The Afghanistan and Iraq invasions and the events since have
merely emphasized the moral and political bankruptcy of the leadership
of the country. What is really unforgivable is, the American people for the
most part have not risen up against the ineptitude and indurate moral
character of their leadership, but have rather passively accepted it as a
matter of course. And then there is an element of the population that has
not only accepted the horrendous nature of American policies and actions abroad, but has chosen to support them in the most ardent fashion
despite their destructiveness.

I can't help but contrast the call we received to support the war effort
after the Japanese attack on Pearl Harbor to George W. Bush's call to the
nation after September 11, 2001. What we were confronted with after
Pearl Harbor was total mobilization. Everyone was to sacrifice to support
those going to war. We experienced the rationing of goods and services,
scrap metal drives, victory gardens, and a call to conserve and not waste

in order to make victory possible. After 9/11, because of the sluggish economy, Bush ordered the people to get out and spend their money, go shopping, to keep the economy running, to show the world who really was Number One by how fast we could recover from the shock. There seemed to be a complete disconnect between the effects of the exercise of U.S. hyper-power abroad and the smooth operation of American consumerism at home.

With the abolition of the draft, the armed forces no longer constitute a basic civilian corps to which most Americans have some attachment. Instead, it has become a mercantile force recruited through the inducements of concrete economic and social benefits, papered over by a strong layer of patriotic propaganda complete with numerous flags and ceremonies commemorating the courage and sacrifice being made by our "Brave Warriors." Unfortunately, these warriors, because of the increasingly inequitable performance of the economy, come from the lower income brackets, and a disproportionate number are recruited from minority groups—especially of color.

DOMESTICALLY, THE BUSH II YEARS have been noted mostly for the huge financial bubble that was created and finally burst in 2007-2008, with disastrous consequences for millions of Americans, many of whom lost their homes, their jobs, and income as well. I am always amazed at how many Democrats refused to take any responsibility for the result of policies adhered to under the Clinton Administration, most notably the repeal of the Glass-Steagall regulatory system which had existed since the 1930s and separated "normal boring banking from exciting speculative banking." This, coupled with the passage of the Financial Services Modernization Act of 1999, opened the way for the creation of all sorts of innovative financial instruments and abusive forms of financial speculation and manipulation. This, combined with the increasing allowance of cheap consumer credit to make up for the decline in real income experienced by much of the population, along with huge increases in military expenditures to cover the costs of the Afghan and Iraq Wars, account for the years of economic fantasy under George W. Bush and for the ultimate crash and confrontation with reality that followed.

I need say a bit more about the consumerist debauchery of the G. W. Bush years. In a sense, I think the rampant consumerism had its origins in the attitudes of those of us who lived through the Great Depression and WWII. We often had to do without things that were essential—food, shelter and clothing, let alone indulge ourselves with such extras as fancy clothes, numerous toys and dolls, and late model cars. We often said to ourselves, "Well, I didn't have these things, but my kids certainly are going to." And so we gave the kids all sorts of things of dubious value. That attitude was passed on to subsequent generations and expanded. Easy credit dulled people's sense of responsibility. Gone and forgotten was the old Scot's dictum, "Son, for every dollar you are in debt, you are that many times someone's slave."

The financial collapse of 2007–2008 gave rise to all sorts of speculation about its impact on the nation and the political course which was to follow. Comparison was frequently made to the crash of 1929 that gave rise to the Great Depression. That comparison was not terribly apt, but did have some merit. What followed 2007–2008 was called "The Great Recession." Initially, many people felt there would be a resurgent uprising from below, as was the case in the 1930s, and a strong demand for fundamental reform to mitigate the effects of rising inequality, which had become especially pronounced in the past 30 years. The nomination of Barack Obama, an African-American, for the presidency of the United States at the Democratic National Convention in 2008 seemed to confirm that assumption. How far the country seemed to have come! How could it be that predictions of fundamental change in the nation's direction could prove to be so very inaccurate?

I DIDN'T VOTE FOR BARACK OBAMA IN 2008. I voted Green, as I had in every election since 1996, with the exception of Kerry in 2004. (I actually supported Kerry—an action of which I am quite ashamed.) Like most people of liberal/left bent, I was fascinated by Obama's meteoric rise to political prominence. I read his book, *Dreams from My Father: A Story of Race and Inheritance* (1995), and was very impressed by the deep, human feelings expressed therein. However, when I read his book, *The Audacity of Hope: Thoughts on Reclaiming the American Dream* (2006), I came away with vastly different feelings. The book was full of glittering populist generalities, but nothing that I could detect in the way of a concrete program to deal with the nation's underlying problems—rising inequality, drugs, mass incarceration, deportations, crumbling infrastructure, health and education. His election campaign of 2008 merely reinforced that skepticism.

I couldn't help but marvel at the way some of my Liberal Democratic friends expressed their disappointment in Obama. Some actually shed tears of joy at his election. They believed a new age was being born. I recall one elderly woman who, judging from the look in her eyes, had fallen deeply in love with him.

There should have been no illusions about Obama. He obviously was a political opportunist, and 2008 presented a very opportune moment. This country—America, the greatest of all nations, the pioneer of freedom and democracy, exponent of human rights and compassion—had been caught during the eight years of the administration of George W. Bush engaging in some of the worst human rights abuses imaginable. Those eight years revealed America to be an overweening imperial power bent on pursuing its dominant role by whatever means available, ignoring fundamental moral precepts in order to obtain the desired results, whatever they might be. In 2008, the country needed a new face to provide some degree of cover for the wrongs that had been committed in the preceding eight years. To the political establishment and its corporate sponsors, Obama seemed to provide exactly what was needed—a dynamic new face of color to provide credence to America's ideology of freedom, democracy, tolerance, and opportunity for all.

Any illusion people may have had that Obama would introduce fundamental reforms to combat rising inequality should have been dispelled early on. He surrounded himself with political hacks like Rahm Emanuel and Arne Duncan from his hometown Chicago, who along with political leftovers from the Clinton years, like Larry Summers, were to be his closest advisors and hold some of the most important posts in his administration. When Obama was confronted with the abuses of the Bush years, he said he didn't intend to look back. His failure to confront those abuses and make a clean break with them meant, in effect, those abuses would continue to haunt the nation into the indefinite future.

Obama entered office in 2009 confronted by the consequences of the financial collapse of 2007–2008. Millions of people lost their homes and their jobs, while others experienced a substantial cut in income due to the rapid decline in business activity. Joblessness passed 10 percent—the worst since the Great Depression. The "Great Recession" was on.

All was not lost. The Great Recession in no way matched the collapse of 1929 and the Great Depression with its extensive homelessness and unemployment rate of 25 percent. Indeed, the financial collapse of

2007–2008 did seem to open up the opportunity for fundamental social and economic reforms such as occurred during the depression years of the 1930s.

People were angry and aroused. I participated in a number of demonstrations during the Great Recession. One of the slogans I remember chanting was, "The banks got bailed out! We got sold out!" "We," of course, referred to 99 percent of the population; "the banks" to the elite 1 percent. Regardless of its limitations, the slogan outlined with remarkable clarity the dominant characteristic of the Obama Administration. Primary concern was for the large banks and corporations. The people would be secondary.

In April 2009, Obama met with the executives of the largest banks and stated that his administration was all that stood between them and "the spears below." The meaning was clear. The widespread anger which was boiling up throughout the country demanding fundamental changes in the banking industry would threaten the power and prestige of those who controlled it. The banks could have been nationalized, or allowed to go into bankruptcy, and the system reconstructed with more emphasis on small, state and local banks, which could be more easily monitored.

There is no indication that Obama had any such things in mind. There was no real effort to prosecute bank executives for their criminality and malfeasance. Instead, for the most part, after the bailout, bank executives continued to get their million-dollar bonuses and enjoy the special privileges that came with their enhanced status. I couldn't help but contrast this treatment with what happened to some of the bankers after the crash of 1929. Some committed suicide, while others—like the head of our own insolvent bank—were prosecuted, convicted, and sent to prison for the crimes they had committed.

Obama did not create any massive bailout program for the suffering people, as was the case under Franklin Delano Roosevelt. Whatever efforts were made to keep people in their homes were pretty feeble. True, unemployment insurance was increased and there was a stimulus package, but while these measures did mitigate some effects of the recession, they were inadequate. While, technically, the recovery began in June 2009, it was scarcely noticed by most people.

WHAT I REMEMBER MOST ABOUT THE GREAT RECESSION was the "Occupy Movement," a protest against the favoritism provided the banks and large corporations, and the failure to significantly alleviate the suffering of the homeless and jobless. While the Occupy Movement originated in New York as a protest against Wall Street, it soon spread throughout the country. My wife and I participated for a while in a mini Occupy Gresham Movement. I also took part in a large one in Portland, Oregon. I think the Occupy Movement reached a peak in size and potency in 2011 or 2012, before a nationally coordinated crackdown shut down the public encampments. Though it gradually faded away, the movement left a lasting impression concerning the urgent need to understand and address the basic causes of the rising inequality and homelessness—an uncaring capitalist system that favors the enrichment of a few over the fundamental human rights of the many.

I need make a few observations about the persons involved in the Occupy Movement. By conservatives, they were often branded as human refuse—drug addicts, lazy bums unwilling to seek gainful employment, petty thieves, and so forth. I had occasion to mingle with Portland occupiers in their encampment in the parks off Fourth and Main Streets in Downtown Portland. True, there were some complaints about drug use, and careless, messy habits of some of the occupiers, as well as damage to public property. However, I found a tremendous sense of community spirit among them, as they shared food and drink and engaged in song and story-telling. The bulk of them had experienced some misfortune as a result of the recession—unemployment, loss of a home, inability to pay for higher education or cover medical costs. Among them were some considerably talented artists, writers, and musicians. In a real sense, they reminded me of some of the people I knew during the Great Depression.

ONE RESULT OF THE GREAT RECESSION was the explosive rise of the "Tea Party" and the Radical Right. The basis for this rise was the failure of Obama's policies to quickly improve the economic conditions of the bulk of the population. The radical right accused Obama of trying to impose "socialism" on the country with his stimulus package and the imposition of some rather feeble regulatory reforms on the economy. The Radical Right demanded a return to the principles of "free enterprise," claiming to represent the poor little businessperson who was responsible, in its opinion, for creating most of the nation's jobs. In reality, however, I think much of the strength of the Tea Party and the Radical Right was due to the changing demographics of the country typified by the appearance of a black person in the Oval Office.

Lurking beneath the surface of this rightward movement has always been an element of white racism. There was a feeling, particularly on the part of some white working-class men, that America was no longer the country they once knew, but had taken on a different hew and color and was headed in a direction beyond their comprehension. Behind this drift to the right was a more sinister element, which reminded one of the last days of the Germany's Weimar Republic in the 1930s. Much funding for the ultra-right came from a small group of very powerful, wealthy persons, such as the Koch brothers, with substantial corporate interests representing the antithesis of democracy. So it was in the case of the rise of the Nazis in Germany. The real source of their rise to power came from the backing of powerful, corporate interests who financed them and provided the social and economic basis of their power.

At any rate, the Tea Party and the ultra-right were just an extreme element in the continuous rightward direction the country had taken for the past 30 years. Whatever promises Obama might have made for a change in direction toward a more progressive one were quickly broken. One of the promises he had made was that there would be greater transparency, "a new openness," on the part of governmental agencies, and public access to information as to their policies and actions. That promise was never observed. Instead, there commenced a war on whistleblowers. Obama has prosecuted more persons under the infamous Espionage Act of 1917 than all previous presidents combined.

One of the more infamous of these cases was the prosecution of Private Bradley Manning, now Chelsea Manning. I won't go into details about Manning's personal life except to say she was short, a small person frequently abused by those around her, and had doubts about her sexual identity. She was involved in intelligence work and discovered the U.S. engaged in some of the worst human rights abuses imaginable. One of the more notorious of these actions was a deliberate attack by an Apache helicopter on a group of journalists housed in a Bagdad hotel in which two Reuters journalists were killed. Later, a video of the incident was obtained and widely shown that vividly revealed the gruesome details of the incident. Manning was tried and sentenced to 35 years in prison on the basis of breaking a variety of laws, including failure to follow military orders and the chain of command.

Manning was never given the opportunity to conduct a proper defense of herself, particularly in line with the Nuremberg principles of the International Law Commission of the United Nations, which state that military orders do not offer an excuse for committing war crimes. But at the end of her trial, Manning made a wonderful statement, saying in effect that living in good conscience was more important than facing 35 years of incarceration. One can't help but admire that sort of courage. I am very happy to say Veterans For Peace, including our Chapter 72, was very actively involved in Manning's defense. One of the more memorable occasions was when a group of us closed down the military recruiting center in Gresham, Oregon.

I think the one thing Obama will be noted for more than anything else is the full flourishing of the Surveillance State. This secret monitoring of millions of people has been frequently pointed to as a blatant violation of the Fourth Amendment of the United States Constitution, which protects "persons, houses, papers and effects against unreasonable searches and seizures." What really happened under the Obama Administration is, essentially, the American people, and many people across the planet as well, have been robbed of personal privacy. Again, we might not know what was going on in the secluded quarters of the National Security Agency if it were not for whistleblowers like Chelsea Manning, Edward Snowden, and WikiLeaks founder Julian Assange. Like Manning, they have shown extraordinary courage in disclosing information needed by citizens of this country in order to make intelligent decisions about the course their government should be following. The Obama Administration has shown no mercy in prosecuting people like Snowden and Assange in a manner consistent with the way Manning was treated.

SO WHERE ARE WE AT THE END OF THE YEAR 2015? The Endless War started by George W. Bush drones on. Currently, the war is focused on ISIS—the Islamic State of Iraq and Syria—which consists of an organization of fanatical Muslim fundamentalists who, through militant action, have managed to gain control over large swaths of Syria and Iraq. In addition, their influence has become a magnet for disaffected Muslim youth deprived of a legitimate outlet for their energies and abilities by Western societies. In a very real sense, these youths are a byproduct of a global capitalist system that fosters rising inequality and condemns millions of people to a marginal existence.

In the past few weeks, particularly vicious terrorist acts have been committed in France and the United States, attributed to perpetrators reportedly inspired by ISIS, and so the question of what to do about ISIS has been placed ahead of most domestic concerns, at least for the immediate future. I am not going to discuss in detail the many-sided concerns that this raises, except to reiterate what I have already implied. ISIS and the growth of terrorism by Muslim fanatics is a byproduct of failed U.S. policies abroad, and in particular the Middle East. One astute observer stated, "the best recruiting tool for ISIS and other Muslim terrorist groups has been U.S. drone attacks on supposed terrorist groups and individuals in which hundreds, and most probably thousands of innocent people have been killed." The Obama Administration has gained great notoriety by enhancing drone warfare to a very extensive degree. It is very difficult to determine today how this new type of warfare is being carried out or controlled, since at least part of it is being turned over to private contractors. Private contracting today is an integral part of the military machine. In terms of numbers, there are more people involved in private contracting of military orders than there are actual enlisted personnel in the armed forces. This further enhances the power of the military-industrial complex over every aspect of American life, making very questionable the future of what little remains of American democracy.

Because he was black, the election of Barack Obama seemed to mark a fundamental change in the American political and social system towards greater equality and a more transparent system of governance. As mentioned previously, nothing could be further from the truth. While the bulk of African-American leadership endorsed Obama, and most African-Americans voted for him, the left, the real left—people like Mumia Abu-Jamal and Cornel West—denounced Obama as another Uncle Tom. I think the quotation from West is most apt, that Obama was "a Black mascot for Wall Street." However one may wish to place it, his administration represented direct continuity of policies that had been followed for about the past 30 years.

The purpose of this paper is not to engage in a detailed critique of some set of U.S. policies, but to hit the high points that have struck me personally. I have already mentioned the banking industry, which is an integral part of the Democratic Party and the Obama Administration. One of the things I wish to stress most is the effect of international trade agreements on the stagnating and declining real income of most Americans. I wish to point directly to NAFTA and similar agreements, which have resulted in massive job loss and displacement of persons. There have been large protests like the one I took part in on November 29, 1999, in Seattle, but they had little effect. Obama very much followed Clinton's footsteps when he came up with the Trans-Pacific Partnership (TPP), often referred to as "NAFTA on steroids," which would open "free trade" to a dozen nations around the Pacific Rim (Australia, Brunei, Canada, Chile, Japan, Malaysia, Mexico, New Zealand, Peru, Singapore, USA, and Vietnam). Like other such agreements, negotiations were done in secret. As in the case of other such agreements, little discussion of the ramifications of this agreement for the people of these nations was done in the commercial media. [Note: After seven years of negotiations, a finalized TPP proposal was signed on February 4, 2016 in Auckland, New Zealand, but could not be ratified due to U.S. withdrawal from the agreement on January 23, 2017.]

THIS PART OF MY DISSERTATION would not be complete without some treatment of Obama's social policies and in particular reference to his hometown, Chicago. Two of the Chicago gang he brought with him to the White House, who I wish to pay special attention to, are Rahm Emanuel and Arne Duncan. In the post of White House Chief of Staff, Emanuel was noted for an aggressive, grating style of operation that frequently offended people. Nevertheless, he was effective in keeping things coordinated and making as certain as possible no one or nothing would upset the course of action set by Obama. I am not certain how Emanuel qualified for his work in government, later in Wall Street, and finally as mayor of Chicago, since as a young person he was trained primarily in the arts—ballet, as I recall. Perhaps that training qualified him for the arts of distraction and deception, which he practiced with a high degree of skill. At this writing (late 2015), he is deep trouble as mayor of Chicago. Irate citizens are calling for his resignation and taking to the streets in massive protests against him and his administration, in particular upset over his handling of police matters and interference in the public school system.

Arne Duncan also fits into something of the mold of Emanuel. His parents were academics with connections to the University of Chicago. Duncan attended University of Chicago laboratory schools, which provided him with an education the quality of which was quite above the standards of those most American school children attending public schools experience. Duncan attended Harvard University and earned a BA degree in sociology. Exactly how he became involved in education is beyond my knowledge, but so far as I could determine, he had little or no teaching experience. Somehow, he became Superintendent of the Chicago Public Schools, where he quickly enraged the teaching staff and a wide swath of the community by arbitrary actions with a heavy emphasis on centralized curriculum and standardized testing. He also closed numerous so-called nonperforming schools, which resulted in the firing of many teachers. A basic principle that goes with school closures is, "close a school and you destroy a community." All too often, the local school is the only place where widely diverse members of the community can get together to discuss their problems and the future of their children. The local school is a basic element of democracy.

As if damage to the Chicago schools wasn't enough, Obama appointed Duncan to the office of Secretary of Education, with results similar to those of Chicago but on a national scale. As a result, a national revolt was mounted against Duncan's Common Core Curriculum and standardized testing. The Chicago teachers symbolizing the heart of this struggle have set national standards for democratic unionism.

The premier achievement, supposedly, of the Obama Administration was the passage of the Affordable Care Act, or "Obama Care," as it is commonly known. It is sometimes referred to as Obama's signature achievement, a lasting legacy to leave to the nation upon leaving public office. For many of us who spent all or most of our lives fighting for comprehensive national health insurance that would cover everyone from womb to tomb, this certainly was not national health insurance as we had imagined it. In reality it was a nice big plum for the insurance industry. Comprehensive, single-payer insurance, as exists in most Western European countries, including Germany under Bismarck in the 1880s, was not even allowed a place at the table for discussion.

Serious consideration of comprehensive national health insurance first appeared during the New Deal days and was brought to a head in the early 1940s by the extensive lack of physical fitness of many young men being considered for the military draft. World War II postponed national legislation on the subject until after the war was over. When the issue finally came up and was proposed as serious legislation before Congress, it was quickly shot down by the usual culprits—the American Medical Association, the drug companies, and the insurance industry.

One additional remark is in order on Obama's human—or, one might say, inhumane—policies. He has deported more persons than any president in United States history. Here we are in early 2016 and another massive roundup of illegal aliens is underway. As in previous cases, they are largely from lands south of the border. I experience a great feeling of outrage when I hear the litany of tragically broken families and extreme violence these people are fleeing. Much of the source of the violence, of course, comes from the military and police forces largely trained and equipped by the United States, which are supposed to maintain law and order, but are used in fact to protect the corporate and business interests in which U.S. concerns have a large stake.

Things are changing. Obama's America is being challenged from several directions. Most significantly has been the rise of the Black Lives Matter movement. The African-American community has always been subject to indiscriminate police brutality and shootings—police assassinations, if you will—but I don't think the African-American community has ever been so united and determined to put an end to it as they are today. Black Lives Matter is a genuine movement, and is not likely to disappear. Quite the contrary, I would expect it to become an integral part of a larger movement to deal with social and economic justice, catastrophic climatic change, and to establish a truly democratic form of governance.

SO NOW I HAVE REACHED THE REALLY HARD PART of this project and that's how to end it. The title I selected was "American Fascism." So now, we are back to where we began: the question, "What is fascism?" Again, I am going to accept the definition the originator gave it, that of Benito Mussolini. It's when the corporations and the government come together. I am going to remind the reader that it's far more than that. Fascism always has a mythology interwoven with it. In Italy, it was the Sons of the Wolf Legend, along with the history and traditions of the Great Roman Empire. On the political side were the corporations, the social and economic elite, and, of course, the military, occupying an enhanced position as the strong right arm of the regime in collaboration with the political organization, the Fascist Party, headed by the charismatic leader, Benito Mussolini. This leader was necessary to crystallize the edifice and set it in motion.

We could construct a similar analysis of Germany, the Third Reich, Hitler, and the Aryan Race, or Japan, with Emperor worship, but that would be redundant. There have been numerous fascist regimes and each has had its peculiar characteristics, but they have always constituted a synthesis of corporate and government interests, an inspiring mythology, and a dominant military and police apparatus, with a strong leader with his political machine to make the system function as effectively and dynamically as possible. You will notice I left out the word "charismatic." I'm not absolutely certain that such a person is necessary. Certainly, Franco, Salazar, and a number of other such dictators were lacking in that characteristic. Nevertheless, I think my outline of fascism is quite applicable.

So does the American system today really qualify as fascist? I don't think so. I don't think it quite fits the picture, although it may before long. Remember that when Huey Long, "the Kingfish," speculated on that question back in the 1930s, he said, "When fascism comes to America, it will come as pure 100 percent Americanism." He had no doubt about its advent. He used the term "when," not "if."

Our country has many of the characteristics of a fascist state. Certainly, the government and the corporations have come together in such a fast and firm marriage that it is difficult and at times quite impossible to tell where one begins and the other leaves off. Then there is the military-industrial complex, which constitutes such an organic part of the system. Its significance demands special treatment, which I shall cover later. We can never forget that tiny elite at the top of the social pyramid and the dominant role it plays in our society. Always bear in mind that at the end of World War II, we were the most egalitarian of all the Western Nations, and certainly one of the most egalitarian on the face of the earth. Today, we are the least egalitarian of all the Western Nations, and rank way down on the worldwide list.

Now the political apparatus is something else again. I likened it to a Siamese twin: At the top are two separate parties, but at the bottom they are joined together. The two parties, despite some differences, are in agreement that the American system must prevail. The differences are more of a tactical nature than of substance. Though the political system shows some signs of cracking, of disintegrating, there is no clear indication of the direction it might take.

There is no doubt about the position of the military. It may have its problems, but it is the shield that protects us all. In one way or another, all of our lives are joined to it. We must honor the brave heroes who sacrifice so much to keep us safe and secure. We must reciprocate on their behalf by appropriating ever more money to see to it that they have the finest arms and equipment that human beings can possibly devise. In the process, we spend as much money on our military as the rest of the planet combined. We are the world's policeman, and must maintain law and order on the planet.

NOTE: *The following was written just before the Democratic Primaries were decided on June 6, 2016, five months before Trump's election.*

SO FAR, WE HAVE NOT GENERATED the leadership characteristic of a fascist state. Donald Trump has most often been named as the person who might fit that category. He is flamboyant, waving his arms and hands outward, capable of saying anything no matter how outrageous or no matter how much it may contradict what he has said previously. Many of his comments, particularly in reference to Muslims and Latinos, are openly racist. He refused to denounce former Ku Klux Klan leader David Duke. To me, he presents the image of a boisterous, spoiled brat who in one way or another has managed to accumulate an inordinately large amount of wealth. When I think of Trump, I keep thinking of the truism, "You can have a tiny wealthy elite or you can have democracy, but you can't have both."

What Trump stands for is a complete contradiction of what a democracy is supposed to be all about, yet he has attracted a mass following of sorts. How do we account for this contradiction? Trump says, "I want to make America great again." This statement, which implies a return to the past, should automatically label him as a reactionary, not a conservative. There is a longing among a wide segment of the American population for a return to "the good old days." There is a feeling of nostalgia, yearning for simpler times, and something solid to give a sense of security and meaning to people's lives.

In September 2015, I discounted Trump as a potential fascist dictator, but I don't entirely do so now. He has managed to snowball too much support, not just from the Republican Right, but also from the white, primarily male working class. While he has alienated support among people of color, which some observers deem essential for victory in November, opinion polls place him close to Hillary in voter support and indicate he might be capable of an upset victory. Much depends, of course, on voter turnout. Trump can't win against a high turnout of young people and members of the minority communities.

A critical factor is the position of Bernie Sanders. Most polls seem to indicate Sanders would win over Trump, but unfortunately, the Democratic Establishment—the party machine and key figures—are overwhelmingly for Hillary, thus pretty much assuring her the nomination. However, many Bernie supporters still hope for a miracle. The future of his position and influence in the Democratic Party is questionable.

There is no mystery about Bernie's popularity. He has great vigor and determination, and has defied the political establishment, whose motives and methods of operation have provoked the suspicion and hostility of a large segment of the population. But in addition, Bernier has a rather clearly defined social program. Fundamentally, he would pick things up where the New Deal left off 75 years ago. From that perspective, there is nothing radical about what he is advocating. People do want real womb-to-tomb national health insurance, free education from preschool through institutions of higher learning, and reasonable wages so they can afford a roof over their heads and food on the table. They also want to look forward to an old age where they can live in dignity and respect. No one loves a runaway banking and financial service industry.

Bernie has already accomplished something truly marvelous. He has mobilized a huge force of young people. Who knows what this may mean for the future.

Of the three main candidates, I have deliberately left Hillary for last. I believe she deserves special treatment. I have heard a number of people, both on Public Broadcasting and among our members of Veterans For Peace, say that under no circumstances would they vote for Hillary. Now when one considers the ignominy of Donald Trump, why wouldn't one support Hillary, at least as the lesser of the two evils? Well, I also reject Hillary as utterly unacceptable, and here are a few of the reasons. Above all else, she is an establishment figure who has: (a) supported neoliberal trade agreements like NAFTA, CAFTA, and at least initially the TPP; (b) supported her husband in promoting mass incarceration of persons enhancing the prison-industrial complex; (c) received support from Chevron and supported fracking in Eastern Europe; (d) exerted hyper-power in matters abroad, like promoting NATO expansion into Eastern Europe; (e) voted for the Iraq War; and (f) consistently promoted the military-industrial complex, even though, in this election, its status has been out of bounds for serious discussion. There could be many more reasons, but lastly, I'll just say she has been the darling of the banking industry, particularly Goldman-Sachs, and I would expect this to continue, regardless of what she says.

One additional remark about Hillary's great sins: In June 2009, the popular elected president of Honduras, Manuel Zelaya, was overthrown by a coup de'etat, an all-too-familiar Central American story, one that reminded me very much of what happened to Árbenz in Guatemala. The results were similar—severe repression of any opposition to the ruling clique. Especially hard hit was the indigenous population. The reason I bring this up is the assassination of Berta Cáceres earlier this year. Cáceres was co-founder of the National Council of Popular and Indigenous Organizations of Honduras. In contrast to the Latin American countries, Secretary of State Clinton had granted recognition and support to the reactionary makers of the coup against Zelaya, thereby creating conditions ensuring ongoing violent repression of social justice movements. In this sense, I hold her responsible for Berta's death as well as hundreds of other Hondurans.

THE FUNCTION OF THE MILITARY ABROAD is only one part of the equation we call the military-industrial complex. We must always keep in mind the remarks made by General Electric's Charles E. Wilson toward the end of World War II, about the value of a permanent war economy. World War II brought the Great Depression to an end, and completely transformed the U.S. economy, making it perform far beyond the expectations of most anyone. I can't help but think back to my rude awakening to the first post–World War II recession, when I went job hunting in 1949. It didn't last long. The Korean War put an end to it.

We have had a series of recessions since then, the worst of which was the 2007–08 Great Recession, but it didn't lapse into a Great Depression due to continuous high level of military spending. The sluggishness of the economy during the current economic recovery—we are in the seventh year now—is merely indicative of the fact that the military stimulus package is not as effective as it once was.

When one considers the crumbling infrastructure of the United States, which is having such a deleterious effect on every aspect of our lives, the question naturally arises—could not the money being spent on the military, or at least part of it, be used repairing and reconstructing the infrastructure of our country through a massive public works program such as occurred under the New Deal? The answer to this question is yes, such monies could be employed more effectively on civilian domestic programs. Numerous studies have shown this to be true. Military spending is the most wasteful form of governmental spending we experience.

Then why do we go on wasting money on the military when the civilian sector is suffering in such dire need? The answer, quite simply, is the vested interests—that tiny, corporate elite that controls our lives, sees public works programs as a threat to its power and influence. This corporate elite and their minions are much more interested in gobbling up what remains of our public services like schools and post offices than receiving contracts for public works. Military contracting is much more profitable and adds to their power and privilege.

One very sharp warning is in order before we finish this critique, and that has to do with the military organization itself, along with the surveillance organizations like the CIA, FBI, and NSA. We aren't a fascist state—yet—but things could change overnight, given an acute crisis threatening law and order. Such crises do occur, both externally and internally. Always bear in mind, the ultimate threat to democracy is internal, not external. When it comes to an autocrat running the country, I am inclined to think of persons like the former Supreme Allied Commander Europe General Philip M. Breedlove. Breedlove is a much decorated, articulate, attractive individual, someone who could easily send Donald Trump back to the dung heap where he belongs. Breedlove makes a beautiful appearance on the media and is a neoconservative hardliner. The military machine is no longer under tight civilian control, as it once was during the days of the impeccable General George C. Marshall.

DESPITE ALL THE DIFFICULTIES, we need not despair. An awakening is taking place. Not all Bernie's followers, especially those young people, are going to go with Hillary. Concern over the military-industrial complex and everyday problems is being overshadowed by the ominous intensification of climate change. If we don't deal effectively with it, we risk losing everything. Life on earth as we are accustomed to thinking of it will be transformed far beyond our imagination and we, perhaps, as a species, will cease to exist. The scientific evidence is in. We have the knowledge and a window of time—a small window—to deal with it.

The great challenge is how to mobilize the forces of resistance to the established order. As Naomi Klein pointed out so well in her book, *This Changes Everything,* the chances of dealing effectively with climate change within the existing order are nil. We have all sorts of activist groups—labor, environmental, peace, social justice, media reform, health and human services. The concerns of these activist groups overlap, as does their membership. No matter how abstract we look at things, we must deal with them here and now—food, shelter, peaceful neighborhoods, schools, access to health facilities—but we must never lose track of the overall object to transform our society into a truly organic, egalitarian, democratic whole.

ONE LAST THOUGHT—*BERTA CÀCERES!*

What happened to Berta in Honduras exemplifies the U.S. imperium of the last 71 years, encapsulated in the words of John Connally, former Governor of Texas and Richard Nixon's Secretary of the Treasury: "My philosophy is that all foreigners are out to screw us, and it's our job to screw them first." [In: Yanis Veroufakis, *The Weak Suffer What They Must?* (Nation Books, 2016), p. 1.]

# Addenda

SATURDAY, NOVEMBER 6, 2016—With this year's presidential election only three days ahead, I must say it will make little difference who wins or loses. The big loser will be the American people. When all the name calling dies away, the American people will be left with a head of state in whom they have little respect or confidence. People abroad will still be appalled by an electoral process that represents little more than a parody of genuine democracy. The great inequities of our society will remain. Major issues—militarism and war, rising inequality, mass incarceration, bigotry and oppression of minorities, crumbling infrastructure, truly affordable health care, free education from preschool through higher education, catastrophic climatic change—were not seriously addressed in the election, and remain to haunt us into the indefinite future.

I can't close without these last few remarks concerning the Clintons. I gleaned much of this information from the November-December 2016 issue of *Mother Jones* magazine, which published an article written by Andy Kroll entitled, "Mighty Morphin Power Player." The article concerns the close relationship of the Sabans, Haim and Cheryl, with the Clintons. Haim Saban is listed on Forbes' ranking of the world's richest persons as 453, worth approximately $3.5 billion. The Sabans have also been the Clintons largest financial backers, having donated about $27 million to various Clinton causes. I don't think this includes many large contributions made to Hillary's presidential bid.

Haim Saban possesses dual Israeli-American citizenship, and as a teenager was a member of the Israeli Defense Forces. After receiving a $2 million donation to her super-PAC, Hillary announced her opposition to the growing Boycott, Divestment and Sanctions (BDS) movement against Israel in protest of that country's human rights abuses. Keep these facts in mind if you expect there might be some effort to alleviate the suffering of the poor Palestinian People on the part of the Clintons.

NOVEMBER 14, 2016—On today's *Democracy Now!* radio show, which I heard on KBOO this morning, Amy Goodman, attending the U.N. Climate Summit at Marrakech, Morocco, mentioned that the Sultan of Morocco, an absolute monarch, gave $12 million to the Clinton Foundation.

DECEMBER 20, 2016—My apologies to those I misled at a meeting of the Oregon Historical Society in September 2015, when I discounted the possibility of a Trump Presidency. Obviously, I was wrong. In a real sense, this brings to an end my long and prolonged dissertation on American Fascism, or what might be termed more accurately, American Imperialism. That very narrow gap between what constitutes an imperial state with a small degree of democratic expression and an outright fascist one is in the process of being closed. Here it is, December 2016, and the forthcoming Trump Presidency is already showing its true colors—those of a racist, bigoted, arrogantly autocratic entity.

This characteristic is being made clear if by nothing else than the initial selection of those who are to be his closest advisors and potential holders of some of the nation's highest offices. As expected, his critics and opponents in the Republican Party have capitulated and fallen into line supporting the Trump Presidency. Indications are that elements in the military-industrial complex are going to do the same.

The psychological effects of the Trump victory are already apparent in the atmosphere of fear and hatred that has been generated. We are entering a period of extreme divisiveness within the nation. Anti-Trump demonstrations are being met by counter demonstrations on the part of white supremacists. Nazi symbols and salutes are coming into vogue. Civil rights and social justice groups are creating sanctuaries for illegal aliens. Many institutions of higher learning are following suit. Indications are that the Trump people will try to eliminate or neutralize such sanctuaries. The grounds are being laid for severe civil conflict in the months and years ahead.

I am not a pessimist about the future. Hillary Clinton's demise is part of the death agony of a moribund liberal class to whom we may say good riddance. Many persons who considered themselves to be on the left as liberals or progressives supported the Clintons or Obama as the lesser of two evils. To support the lesser of two evils is to support evil itself, and to descend down the path into a moral abyss from which there is no exit.

The fact is that the two parties, Democratic and Republican, are not just morally bankrupt, but bankrupt in terms of any program designed to meet the needs of the masses of people in this country or anywhere else on this planet. They have but one common purpose—to serve the needs of the capitalist system and to facilitate its exploitation of the resources and creatures of this planet and most particularly the human community of which we are all a part. Capitalism may be the most creative system ever devised by humans, but it is also the most destructive. Given the "Great Acceleration" of the rate of environmental destruction since the end of World War II, what we are essentially faced with is ecocide. We should never forget that at the heart of the Great Acceleration is the military-industrial complex that is the engine of the economy of the United States. Militarism and war have both been beyond serious discussion by the two major parties. Considering the history and reality of the two parties, particularly during the past 40 years, why would any normal, rational person support them?

As has been the case in every election since 1996, with the exception of 2004, I have voted Green. I think the 2016 Green Party candidate for the presidency, Jill Stein, is a person of exemplary character, a judgment I would also bestow on those around her. The Green Party platform of universal free health care and free education from preschool through institutions of higher learning has been part of every progressive program, from the New Deal down to the present. Stein's advocacy of a program to convert our energy needs from fossil fuels to truly renewable sources in the shortest possible time, to meet the challenge of global warming, is truly commendable. Such a program would create a demand for millions of highly productive jobs. Stein indicated that the cost of such a conversion would be met by slashing the military budget in half and engaging in a whole-hearted pursuit of peace. This certainly would be a gigantic step forward toward the construction of a rational foreign policy. Greens have also advocated other programs concerning taxation and the utilization of public resources that would make for a much more egalitarian society.

While Green Party support tripled in 2016 over what it received in 2012, it fell far short, I think, of what it should have been. The Greens have shown a lack of really good organization. I have contributed a number of times financially to the party, but received no real follow-up. Furthermore, if they have been holding meetings in Multnomah County, I could not locate them on the Internet or any other media. Finally, while the Greens seem to be the logical heirs to the New Deal and Great Society, I don't believe they have any clear perspective on the exigencies of the present time and the need for intelligent, highly trained organizers to deal with it.

WHAT WE NEED TODAY IS NOT SOME KIND of Sanderist political revolution from below, but a genuine social revolution which will alter the entire axis of society—political, economic and social—and establish one of a truly egalitarian, democratic nature. The fact is, we don't even have what constitutes free and fair elections by International Standards. By International Standards, I am referring to those established by the Interparliamentary Group formed in Paris, France, in 1993, and the Carter Center. I am not going to elaborate on the inanities of an electoral system that can put a billionaire like Donald Trump into the White House without receiving a majority of the popular vote. The famous saying, "You can have democracy or you can have great wealth, but you can't have both," applies now as never before. No matter who is elected president, the masses of the people—that figurative 99 percent—are bound to lose. The gap between the rich and the poor will continue to grow. Rising inequality is built into the system. Another old adage applies, "Let me establish the rules, and I will determine the outcome." When all is said and done, people of great wealth and position—that tiny elite, probably considerably less than 1 percent, more like .01 percent —in one way or another establishes the rules that keep the system working in their favor, not that of the masses.

In a real sense, our society functions as a unitary whole with all parts and elements heavily interdependent, exerting their influences on each other. Parceling the system into isolated elements, commonly referred to as reductionism, can really lead to no effective action to change the system.

Now if the revolution I describe sounds like Marxism, fundamentally it is, or at least so far as I understand it. At any rate, I have come out of the closet and will not deny what I am and have been for some time—a socialist. Furthermore, I have been heavily influenced by Marxist methodology, and consider it an essential tool for analyzing society and charting a course of action. I must say I am heavily indebted to the editors, writers and intellectuals of *Monthly Review,* an independent socialist magazine. I was fortunate in reading the first issue in May 1949, which contained a lead article by Albert Einstein entitled, "Why Socialism?" I have been an avid reader and supporter of the magazine ever since. I feel especially indebted to he current editor, John Bellamy Foster, and associates, for developing the concept of "ecosocialism" as a response to the deepening crisis brought on by global warming.

NOW ALL THIS BRINGS US BACK TO THE CONCRETE PROBLEM of how we deal with the conditions we are facing today. There really is a socialist alternative. The problem with Bernie Sanders is he did not go far enough. I don't really believe the Democratic Party can ever be reconstituted in any fashion that will offer a viable alternative for dealing with the increasing inequality that is not just a national problem but international as well. The Democratic Party under the Clintons and Obamas certainly has not been an instrument of peace. Bernie's brutal treatment during the 2016 primary season by the Democratic establishment certainly should have convinced him that reforming the Party was a hopeless task. He would have had a better chance by bolting the Democratic Party and working out a viable alternative with the Greens. Such an event would be bound to upset not just the establishment of the Democratic Party, but possibly the Republican as well.

Yes, there is a socialist alternative, and a clear example of it has been provided by Kshama Sawant. Who is Kshama Sawant? She is a very bright, sophisticated Indian immigrant and activist who was elected to the Seattle City Council as an outright socialist. Her program included such things as the $15 minimum wage, low-income housing, universal free health care, free education from preschool through higher ed, millionaire's tax to cover the costs of lower mass transit fares, support for co-ops and small businesses, and a variety of other things associated with the drive for a truly Democratic Socialist Society. Kshama is one of those remarkable persons who was trained as a computer engineer, then went on to earn a Ph.D. in economics. She has taught in institutions of higher learning. Most importantly, she has shown a solid commitment to improve her community and the world beyond.

Kshama, of course, does not work alone. She has joined with a considerable number of other young people who are intelligent, highly motivated, and determined to meet the challenges posed by global warming and rising inequality caused by the greedy and destructive nature of the capitalist system. These energetic, talented people are organizing work at the community, national, and international levels to transform the system, to rid the world of the destructive capitalist system before that system destroys life as we have known it on this planet. I am convinced the socialist alternative probably offers the best hope for the future and plan to start working with it in the near future.

WHEN I THINK I HAVE FINALLY FINISHED this dissertation, I find I have not. Perhaps I never will. What prompted this addition was a little excerpt from the epilogue of Matthew Josepheson's book, *The Money Lords*. The excerpt was a reference to an article by Dr. Harold Lasswell in the January 1941 issue of the *American Journal of Sociology*, entitled "The Garrison State." In that article, Lasswell depicts the evolution of the United States into a tight military dictatorship very much on the style of Mussolini's Fascist Italy. Now this is very much the theme of my memoir, *American Fascism*, in which I have attempted to bring together the experiences I have had over my lifetime as part of that America. The only thing that has been missing is the eradication of the last feeble remains of what was once a vibrant democracy.

IN SEPTEMBER 2015, at a meeting of the Oregon Historical Society, I was wrong in writing off Donald Trump as a potential president who would close the very small gap containing a bit of democracy in this country and thus convert it into a fascist state. Instead, I pointed to someone more akin to the task. That person was General Philip Breedlove, Supreme Commander of the Western Forces.

In a sense, I think I was basically right in my projection. My thinking was very much along the lines of Harold Lasswell's back in 1941, before the military-industrial complex was fully developed. I also think I was right in discounting Trump as a potential fascist dictator along the lines of Benito Mussolini. Trump lacks the focus, the decisive thought and action essential for a fascist dictator.

However, among his appointees, he does have such persons. In particular, I am going to cite General James Mattis, Mad Dog Mattis, former head of the Central Command. Mattis did not gain the appellation "Mad Dog" for no reason. Certainly, as Head of the Central Command he showed himself capable of coming quickly to firm decisions and acting decisively upon them. The extreme violence he was responsible for in Iraq justly earned him the name, "Mad Dog." Frankly, when I found

Trump was determined to appoint Mattis as Secretary of Defense without having satisfied the normal term of ten years in civilian service, I was frightened.

Mattis certainly has no trouble in developing a firm focus, but he has that ingrained military mentality which makes him unfit for any high ranking position in civilian government. His appointment as Secretary of Defense is certainly a violation of the basic principle of civilian control over the military. One can cite the fact that a similar waiver of the ten-year time limit brought General George C. Marshall to high-ranking governmental positions, but the comparison of the two men and the circumstances are not apt.

A final remark about James Mattis: He has shown no hesitation in contradicting Trump, and Trump's reaction to this has been very weak. In a sense, this is very good, given the flaky, airheaded mentality of Trump and his vast ignorance of governmental affairs. However, this merely highlights the danger of Mattis' appointment. In the event of a severe crisis, he is perfectly capable of taking control of governmental affairs and quickly imposing a military dictatorship. My contention all along has been that the fundamental threat to what remains of American Democracy comes not from some elected civilian official, but from someone within the military with discipline and experience in controlling wide areas of country and population. The only thing we can be certain of is that there will be severe crises facing us in the future, whether they be from extreme internal contradictions, or external ones stemming from foreign relations, climate change, or a combination of all of these things. The opportunity for the imposition of the Garrison State will be there. What's lacking is a countervailing force of a United Left determined to transform society into a truly egalitarian, democratic one. The challenge facing all of us today is to build such a thing.

A NOTE OF APPRECIATION: The mention of Harold Lasswell brings back a flood of memories from my early student years, names like Thorstein Veblen, Max Weber, C. Wright Mills, Bertold Brecht, Karl Marx, Freidrich Engles, Sigmund Freud, Rosa Luxemburg, Bronislaw Malinowski, Ruth Benedict, and Margaret Mead.

But most of all comes back the vision of dear Dr. Wilmeth, Professor of Sociology and many other things at Central Washington State. Dr. Wilmeth took time out of his very busy schedule to meet with a small group of us students in his office, the picture of which, despite the passage of time, remains firmly fixed in my mind—Al Benson, Phil Parker, Molly P. Huston, my great roommate Tom Wiegert, and myself. Dr. Wilmeth gave us a brief acquaintance with the German language, but more importantly gave us the basis for understanding the social-psychological development of human beings, and a much clearer personal understanding of ourselves.

What I owe most to, however, is the G.I. Bill of Rights, which sent me off to that wonderful small community of academics and scholars and gave my life the force and direction it needed. What I received should be the right of every young person today. It is one of those things for which we must continue to fight.

JUNE 22, 2017—What prompts this additional note on American Fascism is the receipt, a few days before my 91st birthday, of a set of internet printouts from my son-in-law, Scotty Somohano, two of which I considered to be the greatest birthday present imaginable. The two articles were from *The New York Times*. The first one was entitled, "American Fascism, in 1944 and Today." The article was published on May 12, 2017, and was written by Henry Scott Wallace, grandson of Vice President Henry A. Wallace. The article concerned a piece his grandfather wrote, entitled, "The Danger of American Fascism," published in *The New York Times* on April 9, 1944. Henry A. Wallace wrote the article in response to three questions posed to him by the Times: (1) What is fascism? (2) How many fascists have we? and (3) How dangerous are they?

The reason for my great joy upon receiving those articles is that I have always considered Henry Agard Wallace to be one of the finest men this country ever produced. He was first and foremost an agronomist and a devoted public citizen. Unfortunately, his many accomplishments have been largely ignored or inaccurately covered in many historical accounts. My own opinion is that if he had been selected as President Roosevelt's vice-presidential running mate in 1944 instead of Harry S. Truman, we would have avoided many of the post–World War II catastrophes and inherited a much more peaceful, equitable, and democratic world.

In 1944, Henry A. Wallace was favored by an overwhelming majority of Democrats, about 65 percent, for a second term as vice president. That he was not selected as vice presidential candidate was due to his dislike by the Democratic Party Establishment and the Byzantine nature of the 1944 Democratic National Convention. Instead, Harry S. Truman, a product of the Pendergast Kansas City Political Machine and a favorite of about 2 percent of the Democrats, was selected.

Basically, the content of these two articles by the Wallaces confirm the substance of my dissertation on American Fascism. The basis of American Fascism is a reality deeply imbedded in the structure of American society as it has developed from the end of the 19th Century down to the present time. If you wish a really detailed account of that reality, you might consult the June 2017 issue of *Monthly Review* magazine, which contains two articles giving the best analysis of American Fascism that I have run across.

In the packet with the two articles my son-in-law sent me was a third article that pretty much dovetailed my preceding remarks—a speech given by Dwight D. Eisenhower before the Society of Newspaper Editors on April 16, 1953. That speech is commonly referred to as the "Cross of Iron" speech, and really constitutes a response to the death of Joseph Stalin, with the resultant feeling of insecurity in world affairs about what was to follow.

The Cross of Iron speech was a wonderful sounding affair full of hopes for a peaceful, prosperous future. This future was to be based on the value system espoused by the Western Nations under the leadership of the United States. That system of freedom and democracy would be opened up to all nations of the world and they would be encouraged to join and enjoy the openness and democratic rights of the Western Nations.

There was only one problem with this vision—the Russians. The Russians seemed intent on expanding their power and influence throughout the world through subversion and the use of force. If only they would join together with peaceful, freedom-loving people everywhere, everything would be fine.

Now, essentially, the Cross of Iron speech is another Cold War document, but it is most important because it was given at the peak of U.S. power and influence, and given by a person who violated the strictures of strict subordination of the military to the civilian branch of government that had been in place since the administration of Ulysses S. Grant.

I'm tempted to go into a lengthy comparison of the character of President Dwight D. Eisenhower to that of General George C. Marshall, but will limit myself to a few remarks. Eisenhower was a great general, and

Marshall's protégé, but certainly did not have the vision and impeccable character of George C. Marshall. Few if any military people did. While Marshall, with the consent of Congress, did serve in the government, he maintained strict subordination to civilian rule. He even refused to vote in elections. There was one exception, and that was over Truman's decision to recognize the State of Israel in 1948. At that time, Marshall was Secretary of State, and Truman's decision to recognize the State of Israel would violate the better judgement of the best informed minds in the State Department on Middle Eastern affairs, and Marshall's as well.

Eisenhower, on the other hand, chose to pick the political alternative of the highest office in the land. At the time, it wasn't certain which political party, Democratic or Republican, would nominate him. He could have had either, but after the Truman Administration, the Republican Party looked the better choice. The Republican Party was backed by prominent persons in the corporate establishment and very well funded.

At this point it is interesting to compare the Eisenhower Administration to the values of freedom and democracy outlined in the Cross of Iron speech. His administration covered eight years of the "Golden Age of Capitalism." His administration has sometimes been called "the administration of the generals"—Charles E. Wilson of General Electric, and Charles E. Wilson of General Motors. Along with them, other corporate leaders of America were involved, and of course their minions.

Among the minions, I must again mention the two brothers, John Foster Dulles and Allen Dulles. The Dulles brothers were corporate lawyers involved in everything from tobacco to sugar. John Foster served as Secretary of State, and his brother Allen headed the CIA. Under their guidance, the democratic regime of Jacobo Árbenz in Guatemala was overthrown, resulting in the death and destruction of tens of thousands of persons, including a huge number of indigenous. A similar thing happened to the regime of Mohammed Mossadegh in Iran in 1953. A whole litany of such events took place under Eisenhower's tutelage.

These nefarious events were epitomized in 1960 by the infamous U-2 incident. Eisenhower's CIA had been sending U-2 spy planes, which flew far above the Russian capacity for flight, to meticulously photograph strategic sites in Russia. The Russians were very much aware of this, and demanded that such flights cease. Eisenhower, of course, denied that any such incursions were taking place. Unfortunately for Eisenhower, the Russians were able to shoot down one of these planes and took the pilot,

Francis Gary Powers, prisoner. Now, I can't help but recall a cartoon in, I believe, *The Oregonian,* depicting Eisenhower with a huge black eye over the incident.

The U-2 incident brought to an end some promising negotiations the U.S. had begun with the Russians. Furthermore, it destroyed the new openness of Nikita Krushchev's government and greatly strengthened the hard-line opposition in Russia.

Eisenhower's final famous speech, given shortly before leaving office, contained a warning about the rising influence of the military-industrial complex. The sad part of that warning is that it came at least ten years too late. Eisenhower never acknowledged, or perhaps was not aware, that he was a product of that military-industrial complex.

Now what does all this seemingly long digression have to do with us today, living under "Trumpism"? The answer is, a great deal. Whatever he may think of himself, Donald Trump is not a free man. He is a creature of the system. There is nothing unique about his position. As a good show-man, he has allowed the ultra-right to play a dominant role in American affairs, at least for a time. But Donald Trump will still have to act and do within whatever the system allows and dictates. Keep in mind, the ulti-mate source of power is the military, backed by those shadowy sources of surveillance and control designed to keep track of all of us, lest we offer some threat to what is increasingly a malfunctioning system. Their power has been consistently increasing, and it wouldn't take much of a shock for them to assume total control of the system.

In this regard, I always keep in mind Harold Lasswell's "Garrison State." We must ever be conscious of the threat of a complete takeover of the state by the military.

Now, I am no pessimist. This is a new era, with a rising new genera-tion. The overwhelming support of Bernie Sanders in 2016 by young people indicates that increasing opposition to the Establishment is what will constitute the future. And not just in this country. The rise of Jeremy Corbyn in British politics, and the outcome of recent French elections both indicate that the rising tide is not just national, but international.

I'm old, but I simply refuse to die, because things are far too exciting!

JULY 31, 2017—What prompted this sequel to my memoir on American Fascism was a brief interview earlier this week on Oregon Public Broad-casting (OPB) with a Democratic governor of one of our states.

Unfortunately, I didn't catch the name of the governor or the state. However, my attention was very much caught when the governor used the term, "counterrevolution." He used it to describe the right-wing assault on the great gains ordinary working people made under the New Deal, and under the Great Society Program of Lyndon Johnson. We are, of course, talking of things like social security, minimum wage, legal rights for trade unions, and the movement to extend voting rights to minorities and to end racial segregation.

The good governor attributed the growth of the far right, or Alt Right as it is sometimes called, and its assault on the gains which working people have made, to the malicious intent of the Koch brothers and the widespread network of agencies that they have created and supported, like the Tea Party, that have had a major impact on every facet of our lives. He notes this Alt Right has obtained a major influence in the Republican Party.

Now I would have gone a bit further than the good governor in his description of the present-day Republican Party. I like Noam Chomsky's evaluation, which I picked up not long ago on Public Broadcasting. He simply stated, "The Republican Party is the most dangerous organization in history." His reference was primarily to the dominance of climate change deniers and the fact that they have Donald Trump in the Oval Office, with his finger on the nuclear trigger. Essentially, the Republican Party has evolved into a full-fledged fascist organ. So-called moderates like John McCain and Paul Ryan are merely fellow travelers. They can be disposed of at an appropriate time.

Now I have a very serious disagreement with the governor. The counterrevolution did not begin in recent years with the Tea Party and the nefarious right wing promoted by the Koch brothers. The counterrevolution was a natural reaction of the leaders of great corporations and their minions to maintain their dominant position of power, profits, and social and economic control over working people. Remember, the corporation is a top-down totalitarian dictatorship whose primary goal is to protect the interests of the shareholders and to enrich their accounts. Politically the corporate mentality promotes whatever groups may best serve its interests. Genuine grassroots democracy is its ultimate enemy. Always keep in mind Mussolini's reaction when asked what fascism is. He simply stated, it's when the corporations and government come together.

There was a great threat to corporate domination during the 1930s.

That threat stemmed from the rise of a militant trade union movement. At its peak at the end of World War II, nearly 40 percent of working people in private industry belonged to trade unions. Gains made by working people came through hard-won strikes and a sense of solidarity throughout the movement. Police and sometimes the military were used to crush such actions. Bloody encounters were frequent. Labor activists and their supporters were often accused of being communists or fellow travelers in attempts to discredit them. Red baiting and blacklisting of the militants were often commonly employed.

World War II was accompanied by inflation, which cut into people's living standards. There were strikes in attempts to rectify losses caused by inflation. The corporate media labeled such workers as unpatriotic and a threat to the war effort. Actually, strikes and militant activities declined during World War II. In contrast, corporations refused to cooperate until they were guaranteed record-breaking profit margins.

The end of World War II was marked by a rapid conversion to a peacetime economy. This conversion was engineered by Donald Nelson, former head of Sears Roebuck Corporation and Chairman of the War Production Board during World War II. This placed him in a key position for supervising the conversion. The conversion did not come about peacefully. The conversion was accompanied by more inflation and a series of strikes by working people to catch up with the rate of inflation. Also, after the sacrifices necessitated by the war, they felt they were entitled to improve their lot. Corporate America, bloated by war profits and basking in its prestige won by the very successful war effort, renewed its assault on organized labor and working people. The result was a massive anti-labor drive by Corporate America and an effort to elect a congress favorable to it. The effort was successful. The result was a pro-business congress in 1947 that passed the infamous Taft-Hartley Act.

With the passage of Taft-Hartley, a rather peaceful period of labor relations ensued. The next twenty years or so is sometimes called "the Golden Age of Capitalism." People in Europe and Japan were busy trying to recover from the damage inflicted by the war. Economically, the United States had no real competitors, and management could make concessions to labor without hurting the bottom line. In return, labor became apathetic. Well-paid labor leadership, in a sense, became part of the system of management. This leadership could discuss issues of wages, hours, and working conditions with management, and then take back the proposed contract to workers for ratification. Such contracts were usually ratified with little dissent.

The insidious part of Taft-Hartley and the post–World War II period of relative harmony in labor relations was, it broke the important feeling of solidarity among working people. Key provisions of the laws outlawed sympathy strikes, secondary boycotts, and opened the way for the passage of right-to-work laws by states and smaller governmental units. With right-to-work laws, workers were not obligated to join or pay dues into the union representing them, even though they were receiving all the benefits of unionization. This broke much of the sense of labor solidarity and stunted the growth of unionization. Thus began the decline of the labor movement that continues on to this day.

The counterrevolution took a big jump during the Nixon Administration. I'm referring to the infamous memo Lewis Powell sent to the Chamber of Commerce in 1971. Powell was a corporate lawyer and a close adviser to Nixon. Nixon later appointed him to the Supreme Court. Powell was very upset by the popular uprising of the 1960s and '70s. In particular, the assault on corporate malfeasance, especially General Motors, typified by Ralph Nader's Raiders, struck Powell as being little more than a development that would lead to socialism or communism. Powell urged members of the Chamber to act quickly to counter this menace to free enterprise. Members of the Chamber lost no time in following Powell's advice.

The Chamber set up the Business Roundtable to spin a web of pro-corporate and business agencies and entities to take control, or at least exert a dominant influence, throughout the country. The web spun by the Business Roundtable was very effective in turning back the tide of popular democracy. The results are what we have today: the triumph of Donald Trump and the Alt Right.

There should be no question about the nature of the Trump Administration. It is a fascist regime, pure and simple. The Trump Regime is the very thing we fought against in World War II and thought we had eradicated. Instead, the counterrevolution has been very successful and, in a way, we are back to where we were in the 1930s. Now, whether or not that's the case depends on us. We might take a lesson from the Sandinistas in Nicaragua. We need to evaluate our weaknesses, reorganize ourselves, and come back with renewed vigor and determination to win out. That is what will give us victory in the long run.

NOW WITH THAT REMARK, this memo should come to an end, but I feel there are two more things that need to be mentioned. The first is the Russian menace. That thing has been used since the Bolshevik Revolution in 1917 (this year is the 100th anniversary) to instill fear in the American people. Fear is the most effective form of social control imaginable. It distracts people from the real dangers, the internal ones. Yes, the Russians have meddled in our affairs, but so have we in theirs, and on a much greater scale. We intervened in the Russian Civil War (1919–1920) by landing American troops on Russian soil in the far east and in the north, around the city of Murmansk. We aided the contras (sound familiar?) in a vain attempt to stem the tide of revolution and reestablish a semblance of the corrupt old order. The whole period since the dissolution of the Soviet Union has been one of meddling, which includes the reduction of Russia to virtually a client state under Boris Yeltsin in the 1990s.

Now there is something else the Russophobes never mention, and that is the Russian contribution, as our friends and allies, to the victory in World War II. We lost 405,000 persons in the war. The total U.S. civilian population lost at home was six persons, killed on the Oregon Coast by a Japanese balloon bomb. The Russians lost 27 million persons, and had two-thirds of the best part of their country totally devastated. The turning point in World War II was not the allied landing at Normandy in June 1944, but the Battle of Stalingrad fought in 1942–1943. We did not land at Normandy until the Russians had defeated the Germans at Stalingrad, and their armies headed westward. At that point, we really became concerned and went ahead with the Normandy landing. One high-ranking Russian official bitterly remarked, "The Americans fought the war with American money, American machines, and Russian blood."

What is it that the Russians really want? After being invaded three times in 35 years from the west, they want assurance that there will be a neutral, arms-free zone on their western frontier. Such a neutralized zone would significantly ease Russian fears of attack and greatly reduce East-West tensions. There have been several times in the last 75 years when such an agreement could have been reached. Instead, we have pushed Western Power eastward, right into the Ukraine on Russia's front door stoop. America's goal from its inception has always been expansion. That's the way the capitalist system works, and ours has been the most successful one on the planet.

THE SECOND MATTER CONCERNS "THE GARRISON STATE." I'm using Harold Lasswell's term, since he did such a wonderful job outlining it in 1941. The military no longer constitutes the civilian force envisioned by our founding fathers and such as largely existed through World War II. Essentially, today's military is a mercantile instrument designed to protect and promote America's corporate financial interests throughout the planet. Much of it has been privatized through contractors. If Erik Prince, founder of Blackwater Corporation and advisor to the Trump Administration, has his way, most military operations will be privatized.

Furthermore, high-ranking officers no longer retire after 30 years of service to play golf or go hunting and fishing, but act as consultants to elements of the military-industrial complex, or accept jobs as highly paid executives in related institutions. They often become extremely wealthy and part of this country's decision-making elite.

Order is coming to the Trump Administration. This order is being imposed by General "Mad Dog" Mattis, as Secretary of Defense, and General John F. Kelly, as Chief of Staff. As Chief of Staff, General Kelly will control access to President Trump. Kelly was a Marine Corps full general and is used to acting very decisively. As Chief of Staff, he won't suffer "idiots and fools" access to the president. What we are dealing with now is the control of key elements of power within the Trump Administration and country by formerly high-ranking military men. In a crisis situation, and we are bound to have such, these men will act according to their military instincts and impose law and order, military style, throughout the country. The result will be the Garrison State. So be on guard.

# Appendix

SOCIALISM: *Where the principal means of production and distribution are publically owned and operated under the control of the working class. A cooperative commonwealth federation based on genuine, egalitarian principles.*

ONE SHOULD NOT CONFUSE SOCIALISM WITH STALINISM. The leaders of the Bolshevik Revolution in 1917 had no illusions about establishing socialism in the backward, semi-feudal Russian State. They were true internationalists who felt they were paving the way for others who would follow suit—most notably the German and French working class. Unfortunately, they were mistaken in that regard.

Even so, Russia in the 1920s was described by the British Labourite Sidney Webb as a spiritual paradise, but a material hell. Despite material shortages, there was a tremendous flourishing of the arts and sciences. This was largely a byproduct of Bukharin's New Economic Plan, which allowed a wide range of freedom.

By the end of the 1920s, Russia had come under the iron grip of Joseph Stalin. Earlier freedoms disappeared, as did many of the prominent artists, scientists, and writers. Also executed or disappeared were 97 percent of the Old Bolsheviki. A period of reaction had set in. The entire resources of Russia, human and material, were devoted to economic development, under a brutal totalitarian system, in an attempt to catch up with the West. In a sense, the United States was the role model Stalinist Russia wished to emulate. The rank-and-file system of organization, with its special privileges and awards, came to resemble in many respects that of a bourgeois, capitalist state. Stalinism has frequently been referred to as a form of state capitalism. In no way did it resemble a decentralized state controlled by working people, which are the earmarks of a socialist state.

# Personal References

BOOKS

Alexandra, Michelle. *The New Jim Crow: Mass Incarceration In The Age of Colorblindness*. The New Press, 2010.

Bacevich, Andrew J. (Editor). *The Short American Century: A Postmortem*. Harvard University Press, 2012.

Cohen, Stephen F. *Soviet Fates and Lost Alternatives: From Stalinism To The New Cold War*. Columbia University Press, 2010.

Flemming, D.F. *The Cold War and Its Origins 1917–1950, Volume 1*. Doubleday and Company, 1961.

Flemming, D.F. *Struggle for the World: The Cold War from Its Origins in 1917*. Collins, 1965.

Galeano, Eduardo. *Open Veins of Latin America: Five Centuries of the Pillage of a Continent*. NYU Press, 1997.

Hedges, Chris. *Wages of Rebellion: The Moral Imperative of Revolt*. PublicAffairs, 2015.

Lifton, Robert Jay, and Greg Mitchell. *Hiroshima in America: Fifty Years of Denial*. HarperCollins, 1996.

Nichols, John, and Robert W. McChesney. *Dollarocracy: How The Money and Media Complex is Destroying America*. PublicAffairs, 2013.

Viroufakis, Yanis. *And The Weak Suffer What They Must? Europe's Crisis and America's Economic Future*. PublicAffairs, 2016.

Zinn, Howard. *A People's History of the United States: 1492–Present*. Harper and Row, 1980.


ESSENTIAL PERIODICALS

*Monthly Review: An Independent Socialist Magazine* (since 1949; Vol. 1, No. 1. Lead Article: Albert Einstein, "Why Socialism?")

*Mother Jones* (since 1976)

*The Nation* (since 1865)

# About the Author

WILBERT L. "WILL" POOL is a native son of the Pacific Northwest and a product of the Great Depression and World War II. He served as a Navy air crewman during World War II, and in the Navy Reserve for four years after the war.

After World War II, he continued his education on the G.I. Bill. His academic achievements include a BA in Social Science, a Masters of Education in Public School Administration, a Masters in Russian Studies, and three summers at Moscow State University as an International Research and Exchanges Board (IREX) scholar.

Will's work experience has varied from heavy construction to 39 years as a high school and community college teacher. He is an avid outdoorsman, dedicated environmentalist, and very much a social activist. involved in labor organizing, civil rights struggles, and peace action since 1947. He is a lifetime member of Veterans For Peace, Chapter 72.

Made in the USA
Lexington, KY
27 September 2017